PRAISE FOR FOR THE AUTHOR AND *WORLD HISTORY IN 3 POINTS*

'This book would make you fall in love with history. Read it, develop insights and connect the dots.'

– SAM PITRODA, TECHNOCRAT AND ADVISER TO THE FORMER PRIME MINISTER OF INDIA

'A great value-add to develop an overall view of world history. I am amazed how this small but magnificent volume distils almost all the key personalities and events.'

– S.V. RANGANATH, IAS, CHAIRMAN, CAFÉ COFFEE DAY AND FORMER CHIEF SECRETARY, KARNATAKA

'I am spellbound. This is a unique perspective on history.'

– SURESH KRISHNA, CHAIRMAN, SUNDARAM FASTENERS LTD AND TVS & SONS

'Absolutely delightful. History came alive for me through this book.'

– TAMAS LANDESZ, DIRECTOR, WORLD HEALTH ORGANIZATION

'No other book made history as interesting and informative for me.'

– KARINE SARGSYAN, MANAGING DIRECTOR, INTERNATIONAL BIOBANKING, UNIVERSITY OF GRAZ, AUSTRIA

'Zac Sangeeth is already a deep scholar in the subject. I have never met anyone like him.'

– DR V. RAGHUNATHAN, FORMER PROFESSOR, IIM AHMEDABAD, AND ONE OF THE TOP 50 GLOBAL INDIAN MANAGEMENT THINKERS

'This audacious survey of the whole panorama of world history and the narration with such admirable brevity reminds one of great writers like H.G. Wells.'

– ABRAHAM KURIAN, IPS, FORMER DGP, UTTAR PRADESH

'Not just a 2-minute take on any important topic in history, but it's the unique perspective that this book brings. Rekindles your interest in history.'

– SUNIL RAJSHEKHAR, CHIEF EXECUTIVE OFFICER, INDEPENDENT PUBLIC SPIRITED MEDIA FOUNDATION

'Absolutely unique way of presenting history. Well researched, comprehensive, and at the same time precise.'

– FEROSE V.R., SENIOR VICE PRESIDENT AND HEAD OF SAP ACADEMY OF ENGINEERING, USA

'It is extremely difficult to simplify complex subjects. The way this book simplifies history is an absolute work of genius.'

– MIREILLE TOULEKIMA, AWARD-WINNING TALK-SHOW HOSTESS

'If you are not a history buff like me, this book would change that. Perhaps, this is the best book to help one develop a firm foundation in history. It is a far cry from what we have made of this amazing subject in our school curriculums. Give it a try.'

– KISHA GUPTA, DIRECTOR AND GLOBAL HEAD – ACADEMIC RELATIONS, INFOSYS

'I learnt more than I ever did during my schooldays. A thoroughly researched and well-structured book.'

– JIPU JOSE JAMES, EXECUTIVE DIRECTOR, JONES LANG LASALLE

'History can sometimes seem boring - but Zac Sangeeth brings it to life by getting to the heart of every matter in this enjoyable book. It will entertain you - and it will also enlighten you.'

– AMIT VARMA, WRITER AND PODCASTER

'Brilliant. Everything in a nutshell. Most useful for a non-history student.'

– SEBASTIAN EDASSERY, DIRECTOR, DELOITTE

'This book presents vignettes helping you wade through history. It is painstakingly researched and very well written. I have not yet come across any book that crosses civilizations, cultures, events and characters across history and yet manages to connect the dots across time.'

– AMIT GOPAL, PRINCIPAL, MERCER CONSULTING

'Covering world history in a single book is an ambitious and arduous task. This book does it in a greatly admirable manner.'

– CDR JAGAN GIRISABALLA (RETD), CHIEF OPERATING OFFICER, PURPLEFRONT TECHNOLOGIES

'Reading through any chapter of this book feels like going through an instant yet enriching time capsule.'

– SAURABH NANDA, FOUNDER, SN MENTORING

'This book gave me a complete, different experience in understanding history.'

– VIDYADHAR PRABHUDESAI, FOUNDING CURATOR, GLOBAL SHAPERS THANE, WORLD ECONOMIC FORUM

'The presentation, format and delivery is appropriate for the fast paced times we live in.'

– RAJAH RAGHURAMAN, ENGINEERING MANAGER, CATERPILLAR

'*World History in 3 Points* offers a quick but delightful excursion through the major historical events. An interesting experience both for adults who reluctantly studied history for exams and kids who wish to explore this fascinating subject.'

– HARIKUMAR, ASSISTANT GENERAL MANAGER, PUNJAB NATIONAL BANK

'Amazing. This book made boring history super fun.'

– SHEEMA TASNEEM, HR BUSINESS LEADER, INFOSYS

MORE WORLD HISTORY IN 3 POINTS

TO-THE-POINT SUMMARIES OF EVERYTHING THAT MATTERED

ZAC SANGEETH

hachette INDIA

Zac Sangeeth is the author of *World History in 3 Points* (Hachette India 2022) and amongst the world's youngest historians and youngest commissioned non-fiction authors. He strives towards making the subject of history accessible to all – by simplifying it and by making it interesting – through mediums like books, comics and videos.

An enthusiastic public speaker, he has spoken in forums such as the Global Shapers of the World Economic Forum, the Youth Forum, Switzerland, and Lead India, USA. He is passionate about unearthing fascinating 'long threads' from history, on how obscure individuals and events of the past have an unimaginable influence on our present. His most appreciated keynote speeches include:

- Principles and practices from history for a happy, meaningful and successful life
- How a 5000-year-old muddy road in ancient Assyria led to Indian independence
- How pandemics created new world orders and recreated hidden aspects of our lives
- How the desserts we cherish today evolved alongside world conquests and explorations

Connect with the author:

- Twitter: @Sangeethzac
- Instagram: ZacSangeeth
- YouTube: History with Zac Sangeeth

To my amma and appa

First published in paperback in 2022 by Hachette India
This edition published in 2022
(Registered name: Hachette Book Publishing India Pvt. Ltd)
An Hachette UK company
www.hachetteindia.com

SRD

COVER IMAGES CREDITS
FRONT COVER: Ming dynasty seal, Pandya fish symbol, Rod of Asclepius: sourced from Wikimedia Commons; Hunted down deer: sourced from Freepik.com; zigag line pattern: sourced from Freepik.com (modified); Fleur-de-lis by Renee Ramsey-Passmore: sourced from Noun Project/thenounproject.com; Ollin of Aztec, Tanit: Public Domain, modified; ***SPINE:*** Symbol: sourced from Freepik.com; ***BACK COVER:*** Symbols on top of page: sourced from Freepik.com

Illustrations on pages 193, 195 © 2022 Ishan Trivedi
Illustrations on pages 66, 189 © 2022 Ayesha Syed
All maps by Syed Salahuddin © 2022 Hachette India
Photographs sourced from Wikimedia Commons Public Domain
Please see page 245 as an extension of the copyright page.

ISBN 978-93-93701-05-3

Hachette Book Publishing India Pvt. Ltd
4th & 5th Floors, Corporate Centre
Plot No. 94, Sector 44, Gurugram – 122003, India

Typeset by Manmohan Kumar, Delhi

Printed and bound in India
by Manipal Technologies Limited, Manipal

FSC www.fsc.org
MIX
Paper | Supporting responsible forestry
FSC™ C043100

Contents

SOUTH ASIAN EMPIRES

SOUTH-EAST ASIAN AND CHINESE EMPIRES

PERSIAN EMPIRES AND MONGOL KHANATES

AFRICAN EMPIRES

SOUTH AMERICAN EMPIRES

FAMILIES AND DYNASTIES

ARTISTS AND ARCHITECTS

POETS, MUSICIANS AND AUTHORS

SOUTH ASIAN EMPIRES

1 The Pandya Dynasty

The Pandyas of Madurai, as they are also known, alongside the Cheras and the Cholas, formed the three great dynasties of south India. While they may have ruled from 600 BCE, they went through several waves of decline and resurrections: the first revival took place during the sixth century CE and then in the 13th century CE.

1 The Pandyas started out as local chieftains with their capital located in a small village called Korkai in present-day Tamil Nadu. As they began to expand their dominance over the political, economic and sociocultural milieu of the region, they moved to a bigger city, present-day Madurai. During this time, they constructed several temples, made great progress in art and literature, and participated in trade activities, especially involving pearls, spanning the globe. However, the Early Pandyas were soon overthrown by another dynasty, the Kalabhras. Following this, the Pandyas were relegated into obscurity. After several centuries, in 580 CE, they managed to regain power. The Pandya kings of this period successfully vanquished their

rivals – the Cheras, Cholas, Pallavas and Chalukyas. However, by 960 CE, the Pandyas were defeated by the Cholas, driven out of their territories and forced to seek refuge on the island of Sri Lanka. After remaining in exile for around two centuries, the Pandyas re-emerged in 1217 CE, ransacking Chola territories and establishing their second empire.

2 The Pandyas made noteworthy contributions to India's cultural landscape. For instance, they organized large-scale conferences to exchange ideas on Tamil literature, so much so that the legendary Sangams (or 'academies') were held in Madurai under the patronage of the Pandyas. Poets and authors from around the world attended them, resulting in notable works in Sangam literature such as the *Agathiyam*, *Tholkappiyam*, *Silapathikaram*, *Ettuthogai* and *Pathupattu*. The Pandyas also invested heavily in temple projects, such as in the construction of the Kunnandarkoil Cave Temple in Pudukkottai district, the Meenakshi Amman temple in Madurai and the Nellaiappar temple in Tirunelveli. The Early Pandyas enjoyed strong diplomatic relations with faraway regions and boasted an extensive trade network covering regions such as Rome, Greece, China and Egypt. Edicts of Ashoka from the third century BCE as well as the accounts

of Megasthenes, Yu Huan, Pliny, Ptolemy and Marco Polo mention the Pandya Empire.

3 The Pandya Empire eventually declined due to invasions, internal struggles and poorly managed finances. In the early 1300s, a civil war between two Pandya brothers, Parakrama and Kulasekhara, gave one of their allies, Alauddin Khilji of the Delhi Sultanate, a chance to invade. Though the Pandyas sought the help of the Vijayanagara Empire, this led their empire to be taken over.

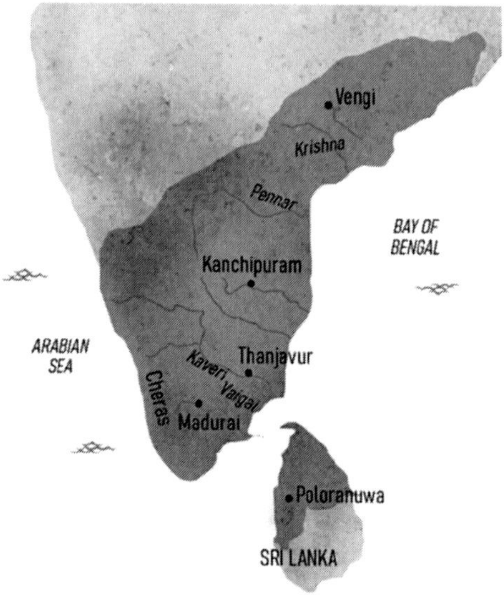

■ PANDYA TERRITORIES UNDER JATAVARMAN SUNDARA PANDYA I (1251–83 CE)

2 The Chola Empire

One of the longest-reigning dynasties in world history, the Chola dynasty originated in the basin of the River Kaveri. They ruled parts of south India from 600 BCE until the 13th century CE.

1 The history of the Cholas can be divided into three periods: the Early Cholas, the medieval Imperial Cholas and the Later Cholas. Remarkably, the Early Cholas are mentioned in one of the pillar inscriptions of Ashoka from the third century BCE. Likewise, *Periplus of the Erythraean Sea*, an ancient logbook, mentions Chola ports and their cities. The Cholas make an appearance in early Sangam literature as well. The medieval Imperial Cholas rose from near obscurity in 850 CE by taking advantage of a conflict between the Pandya and the Pallava dynasties. This enabled them to take over Thanjavur and make it their capital.

2 The Chola dynasty was at its peak during the 10th and 11th centuries CE, during the reigns of great emperors such as Rajaraja Chola I and his

son Rajendra Chola I. At its peak, the Chola Empire stretched from the island of Sri Lanka and expanded to the Godavari–Krishna river basin in the north, spanning the Konkan coast in Bhatkal, and including the entire Malabar Coast. After military and political alliances forged with the Chalukyas, the Later Chola dynasty emerged from 1070 CE onwards. While they managed to conquer many territories, including Kalinga, their power declined from 1118 CE onwards. The Chola Empire erected a strong economy, centred on trade that flourished throughout South Asia, and included China and South-East Asia. The empire was known for its rich culture and legacy in south India. Its architectural influence can be seen in many temples that were constructed during their time, including Thanjavur's famed pyramid-shaped Brihadisvara Temple, adorned with ornate sculptures carved into the walls. The Cholas were also known for their remarkable sculptures and bronze works. The most famous of them is the Nataraja or the Adavallar, depicting Shiva in his divine dance pose. The Imperial Chola era also marked the golden era of Tamil literature, which included

THE BRONZE NATARAJA DESIGN OF THANJAVUR

the production of works such as the *Rajarajesvara Natakam*, *Viranukkaviyam* and *Kannivana Puranam*.

3 The empire started to decline with the second-wave rise of the Pandyas and the Hoysalas. In 1217, the Cholas were defeated by the Pandyas. Though the Cholas managed to win their territories back, their downfall continued, eventually ending one of the longest ruling empires in the world.

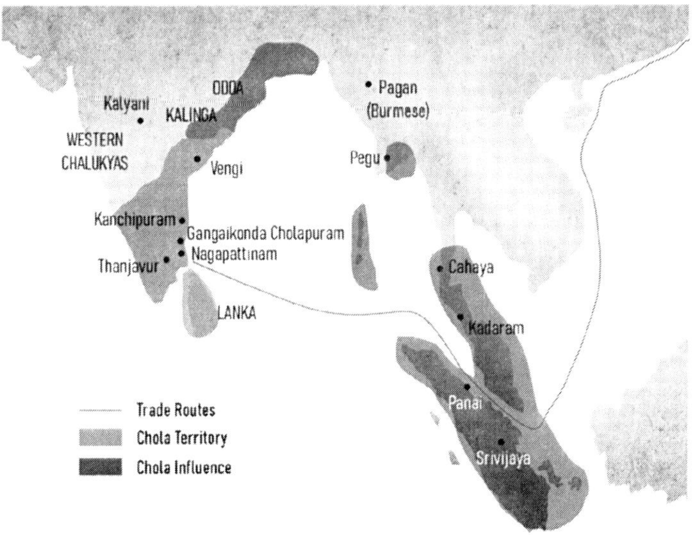

CHOLA TERRITORY AND INFLUENCE

3 The Chera Empire

The Cheras ruled the Malabar Coast of Kerala and parts of Tamil Nadu, with their capital at Vanchi. Their rulers, the 'Keralaputras', ruled from the third century BCE until around the 12th century CE.

1 Like the Pandyas and the Cholas, the Cheras too had a significantly long reign divided in phases. The Early Cheras ruled during the Sangam period, dates for which range from the first century BCE to the fifth century BCE. Around the third century CE, the Cheras were displaced, along with many other kingdoms including the Pandyas, by another dynasty, the Kalabhras. The later Cheras, or the Kulakshetras, appeared during the ninth century CE, and erected a new city, Mahodayapuram. The dynasty's greatest rulers included Senguttuvan and Kulasekhara Alvar.

2 The Chera kingdom flourished, especially due to its trade relations with Egypt, Rome, Greece, the Arabian Peninsula, Mesopotamia and Persia. They controlled the ancient port of 'Muziris', from where they traded in exotic spices, ivory, timber and pearls. They monopolized the production of Wootz

steel, or Seric steel, used to make Damascus blades. Their special style of Dravidian architecture is seen in the Thiruvanchikulam Shiva and the Bhagavathi Amman temples in Kerala, and the Kalambar Koil Temple in Tamil Nadu. They were also known for copper, bronze and clay sculptures of deities.

3 After being defeated by their rivals, the Cholas and the Pandyas, and then due to internal conflicts, the Chera dynasty began to decline from the 11th century CE. Soon kingdoms such as the Zamorins of Calicut, Travancore and Kochi took over their territories.

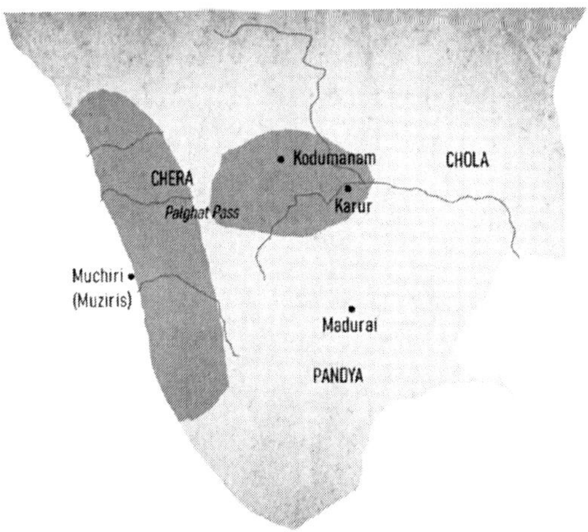

THE TERRITORY OF THE CHERAS

4 The Mauryan Empire

The first empire to consolidate most of the Indian subcontinent, the Mauryan Empire was founded by Chandragupta Maurya. The empire existed from 322 BCE to 185 BCE.

1 In 326 BCE, Alexander of Macedonia made Porus, the king of a small kingdom in Punjab, his ally. However, after Alexander left India, Porus was assassinated by a Greek general named Eudemus, resulting in revolt and the eventual takeover of the kingdom by a young rebel leader Chandragupta Maurya. With the help of his strategist, Chanakya, Chandragupta then raised an army and an espionage network, to defeat the Nanda Empire, which had earlier consolidated the 16 oligarchic republics of north India called the Mahajanapadas. Maurya eventually took over Magadha, the capital of the Nandas, and expanded his kingdom across the Indus Valley and north-western India through a series of campaigns.

2 After Chandragupta, his son Bindusara, who ascended the throne in 297 BCE, extended his rule towards the Deccan Plateau in south

India. In the succession struggle after Bindusara, his son Ashoka 'the Great' took over the empire in 272 BCE. He crushed all internal rebellions and then turned his attention towards Kalinga, a kingdom in east India, the only region yet to be annexed by the Mauryas. Though Ashoka managed to conquer it, Kalinga proved to be a costly war, where both warring factions experienced heavy losses. The sufferings caused by the war greatly impacted Ashoka - he had a change of heart and accepted Buddhism and non-violence as a way of life. He let go of his expansionism plans and invested heavily in public works, built a stable administration, and sent envoys across Asia and Europe. Thereafter, Ashoka's period was regarded as one focused on the well-being of his citizens, and peace and harmony.

CAPITAL OF ASHOKAN PILLAR IN LAURIYA-NANDANGARH, CHAMPARAN, BIHAR

3 The Mauryas brought in a centralized administrative system, a unified military and a single currency across the empire. Taxes were moderated, internal security was established, public infrastructure was built, and trade and commerce expanded during this period. The Mauryan kingdom

declined after Ashoka, due to multiple reasons, including weak successors, internal rebellions and conquests by other kingdoms. There is also a theory that Ashoka's adoption of non-violence could have had an adverse effect on the military's morale and administration since expansionism took a backseat. The Mauryas were replaced by many kingdoms including the Shunga dynasty and the Greco-Bactrian kingdoms.

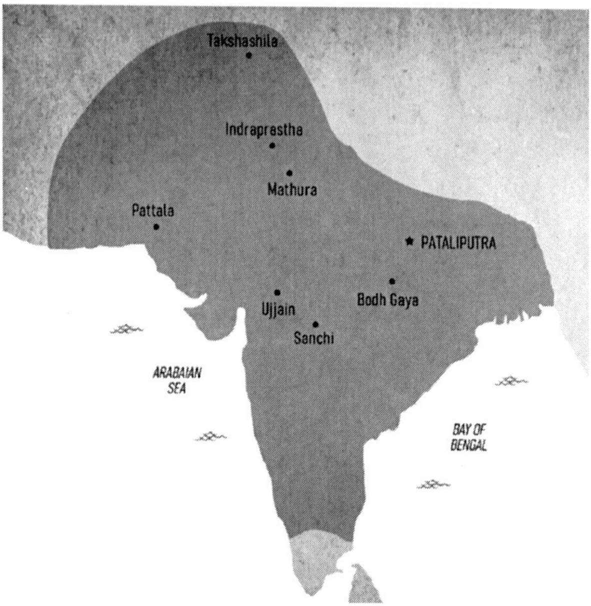

THE MAURYAN EMPIRE

5 The Satavahana Dynasty

The first Deccan-based dynasty to establish an empire in south India, the Satavahanas flourished from the mid-first century BCE to around 225 CE.

1 After the decline of the Mauryan Empire, post Ashoka, many smaller kingdoms sprouted in the Deccan. The Satavahana dynasty was founded at this time by Simukha, who defeated the Kanva dynasty in east and central India. They expanded across present-day Andhra Pradesh, Maharashtra and Telangana, and parts of Gujarat and Karnataka. Their greatest king was Gautamiputra Satakarni (reign: 106–130 CE), who expanded the empire.

2 The Satavahanas are known for agricultural development between the rivers Krishna and Godavari. Paddy was the backbone of their economy. They promoted trade and undertook excavations, unearthing artefacts such as pearls. They are famed for intricate wall carvings and rock temples. Many monasteries were cut from solid rock in their time. While being Hindu Brahmins, they were generous towards other castes and religions.

3 Though the Mauryas ruled over the Deccan during the fourth and third centuries BCE, it was under the Satavahanas that the region flourished, with Indo-Roman trade. However, they started to decline from early 200 CE onwards. The last king in this dynasty was Pulamavi IV.

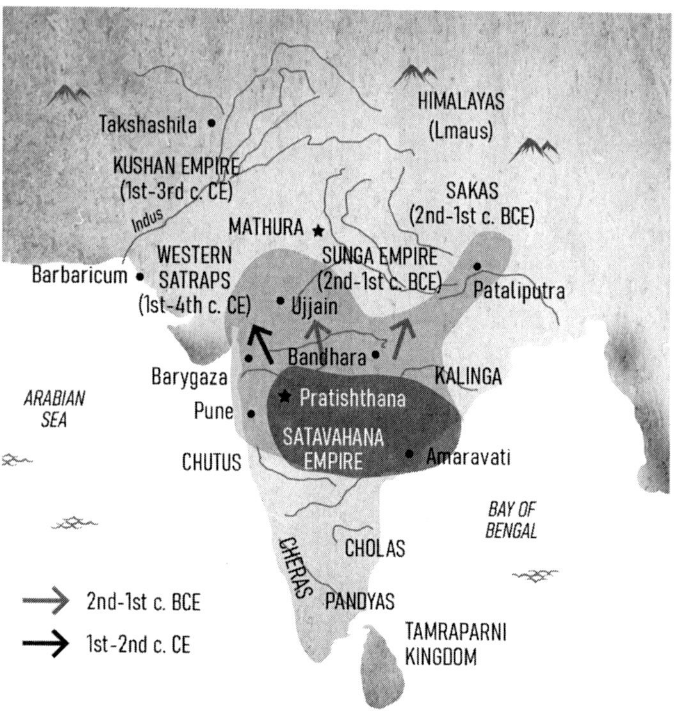

■ THE SATAVAHANA EMPIRE

6 The Gupta Empire

Extending across most of the Indian subcontinent, the Gupta Empire is regarded as the golden age of India. It lasted from 240 to 550 CE.

1 Though the early history of the Guptas is unknown, they might have originated in Uttar Pradesh, India, where they belonged to the Vaishya or the trading class, who rebelled against the taxation regimes of the previous rulers. The empire was founded by Sri Gupta in 240 CE, initially as a small kingdom including Magadha, with Pataliputra as the capital. The marriage alliance of Sri Gupta's grandson, Chandragupta I, with princess Kumaradevi of the Licchavi tribe, which controlled Bihar and Nepal, enabled the Guptas to expand their political power further.

A GUPTA ERA SCULPTURE OF HARITI, A BUDDHIST FEMALE DIVINE FIGURE

2 During the period of Samudragupta from 335 CE onwards, the empire reached its pinnacle. He conquered most of north India and added parts of south India, building a kingdom extending from the Himalayas in the north to the River Godavari in the south. In 375 CE, Chandragupta II became the emperor and further expanded the empire west and eastwards. His reign ushered in the 'Hindu' golden age, where art, literature and culture progressed, especially centred around Sanskrit. He followed a policy of religious tolerance and built several magnificent temples, including Buddhist monasteries. Some of the greatest scholars of the time were advisers in his court, including the poet Kalidasa, author Vararuchi, grammarian Amarasimha and astrologer Varahamihira. The administration was made efficient and trade and commerce flourished during his reign. He also founded a second capital, in Ujjain.

3 After the death of Chandragupta's grandson Skandagupta in 467 CE, the empire started to decline. Its weak rulers were not able to administer the vast territories under an inefficient bureaucracy. There were several domestic conflicts in the ruling family, adding to the disorder. By early 500 CE, the empire was under attack by the Huns,

resulting in its gradual disintegration, giving way to smaller local rulers and independent kingdoms.

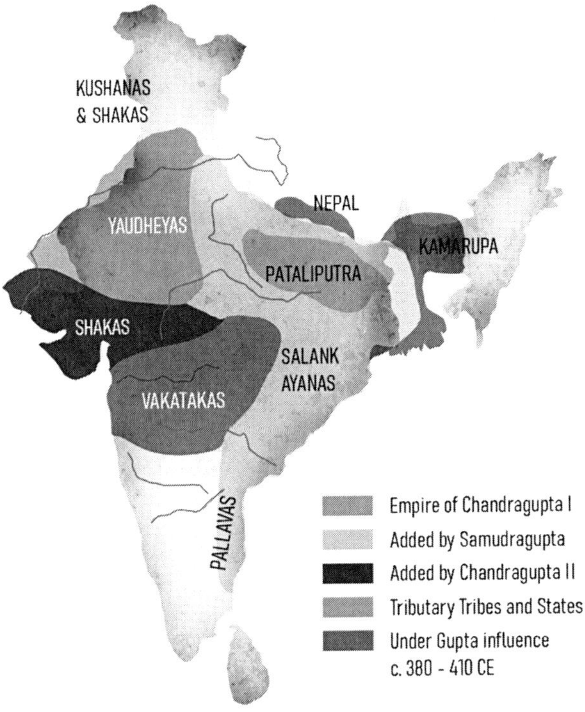

THE GUPTA EMPIRE

7 The Pallava Dynasty

A formidable power in south India from the fourth century CE until the ninth century CE, the Pallavas ruled for about 500 years. Kanchipuram in present-day Tamil Nadu was their capital.

1 Initially a feudal or vassal state of the Satavahana dynasty in the Deccan, the Pallavas moved to Kanchipuram. Here, they managed to capture and consolidate power during the early fourth century CE. They rose to the height of their power by the seventh century CE, when the territories they ruled extended from northern Andhra Pradesh to the River Kaveri. They were so formidable during this period that even the Cholas of the region were reduced to a marginal power. The Chalukyas, another important power in the region, were conquered by the Pallava king Narasimhavarman I (630 to 668 CE).

THE SHORE TEMPLE, MAMALLAPURAM

2 The Pallava dynasty was noted for its contribution to art and architecture. The Pallavas laid the foundation for medieval south Indian architecture, with their vast architectural projects. They followed a special type of Dravidian architecture, divided into two phases. The initial rock-cut phase, during the seventh century CE, mainly contained pillared halls cut out of mountain faces, such as in the cave temples at Mandagapattu in Tamil Nadu. In the second phase of their reign, after 700 CE, free-standing monolithic shrines called 'rathas' (chariots) were constructed alongside pillared halls; a great example is the Pancha Rathas complex in Mamallapuram (Mahabalipuram). The dynasty was also known for its elegant currency system, with coins minted in lead, bronze and copper, beautifully decorated with inscriptions and carvings. The Pallava script developed at this time, later giving rise to several other South-East Asian scripts. Mahendravarman I (reign: 590–630 CE) was a great ruler under whom some of the most intricately detailed monuments dedicated to the Hindu god Shiva were commissioned at Mamallapuram in Tamil Nadu. Though they followed Hinduism, the Pallavas also supported Buddhism and Jainism in south India.

3 The Pallava Empire reign began to decline during the first half of the eighth century CE, despite constructive efforts to keep their three rivals at bay: the Chalukyas, the Pandyas and the Rashtrakutas. During the same time, the Cholas, who were earlier subdued by the Pallavas and made their vassals, started rising again. Soon after, the Chola king Aditya I (871 to 907 CE) managed to occupy Pallava territories. The last ruler of the Pallava dynasty, Aparajitavarman, was killed in battle against the Cholas.

THE PALLAVA KINGDOM

8 The Chalukya Empire

Ruling over most of modern-day south and central India, the Chalukyas had three periods of rule: the Early Chalukyas (from 543 to 757 CE); the Western Chalukyas (from 975 to 1189 CE); and the Eastern Chalukyas (from 624 to 1070 CE).

1 The Chalukya dynasty was established in 543 CE by Pulakeshin I, formerly a petty chieftain, in modern-day Badami in Karnataka, establishing the city as the capital of his empire. These Early Chalukyas, also known as the Chalukyas of Badami, ruled the Deccan, comprising present-day Karnataka and Andhra Pradesh. They withstood the onslaught of rivals, such as the Pallavas, and the Arab expedition under the Umayyad Caliphate. The Western Chalukya Empire, known as the Chalukyas of Kalyani, ruled from 975 to 1189 CE, but declined during the rise of rivals such as the Hoysalas and the Pandyas. The Eastern Chalukyas, called the Chalukyas of Vengi, rose out of the Chola-Chalukya alliance. There were constant battles for power between the Western and the Eastern Chalukyas.

2 The Chalukya dynasty is known best for its rich culture and art. During the Early Chalukyas, architecture flourished and many temples were built in the Chalukyan architectural style: the structure was built in a pyramidical shape and was surrounded by pillars, somewhat similar to the Sangam architecture of the Chola and the Pandya empires. Notable structures of architectural significance built during the Chalukya periods

THE CHALUKYA EMPIRE C. 640 CE

include the Pattadakkal temple town, and the Mahadeva, Mallikarjuna, and Kallesvara temples, all in modern-day Karnataka. The Chalukyas were also known for their ability to mint intricate coins. Unlike other empires, instead of featuring the image of the emperor, Chalukya coins bore images of their temples and artefacts. The Chalukyas are also said to have facilitated the fusion of north and south Indian cultures and ideas, by adopting Dravidian and Nagara styles of architecture together, and by mingling vernacular languages with Sanskrit.

3 Internal strife as well as warring factions led to the decline of the Chalukyas. In the case of the Early Chalukyas and the Eastern Chalukyas, the Rashtrakutas emerged as their main rivals and weakened them considerably. For the Western Chalukyas, their rivalry with the Pallavas led to their decline.

9 The Rashtrakuta Dynasty

Ruling over large parts of south India, the Rashtrakutas flourished between the eighth century and 10th century CE.

1 The Rashtrakuta dynasty was established as a major power by its founding emperor, Dantidurga, in 753 CE. Initially they were just feudatories of the Badami Chalukyas, a dominant dynasty that ruled over most of south India, until Dantidurga overthrew the Chalukya emperor. The Rashtrakutas later conquered some of the stronger empires in India, including the kingdoms of Kalinga and Kosala. At the height of their power, they ruled over present-day Karnataka, and parts of Tamil Nadu, Andhra Pradesh, Telangana, Maharashtra and parts of Gujarat.

2 The Rashtrakuta dynasty took significant strides in agriculture, trade and commerce. The kingdom was rich in mineral resources, and exported silk, jewellery and ivory to regions as far as Persia. They established a unique architectural aesthetic called the Karnata Dravida style, its best

examples being the rock-cut temple complexes of Ellora and Elephanta in Maharashtra. The dynasty mainly followed Buddhism, but also patronized Jainism and Hinduism.

THE ROCK-CUT KAILASANATHA TEMPLE, ELLORA

3 The Rashtrakuta dynasty fell in 972 CE, due to invasion by the Paramara dynasty. Thereafter, a part of their kingdom was annexed by the Later Cholas and other dynasties.

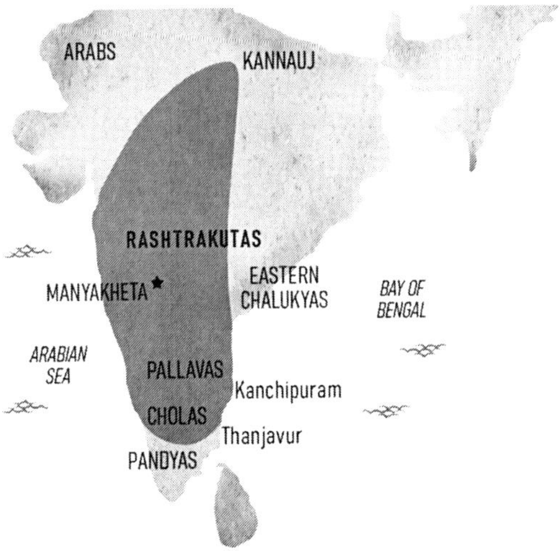

■ THE RASHTRAKUTA EMPIRE

10 The Kakatiya Dynasty

A major power of the Deccan in south India, the Kakatiyas ruled from the 12th to 14th century CE.

1 The dynasty was initially established as a feudal kingdom, serving the Rashtrakutas, and later the Western Chalukyas, both important and powerful empires. The Kakatiyas established their rule under Prataparudra I, who invaded the other weaker feudal kingdoms of the Chalukyas. This weakened the Chalukyas, enabling the rise of another dynasty, the Pallavas, who conquered the Chalukyas. The Kakatiyas conquered almost all of present-day Andhra Pradesh, Telangana and parts of Karnataka, making their empire as large as those of the Chalukyas and Rashtrakutas before them.

2 The Kakatiya period was a golden age of Telugu culture. They encouraged Telugu and Sanskrit literature. They built hundreds of temples in the Sangam style of architecture using pillars, such as the Thousand Pillar Temple and Ramappa Temple in Telangana. They also constructed a network of tanks for irrigation, boosting agriculture.

3 The Kakatiyas were constantly attacked from the north, especially by the Delhi Sultanate. The first two attacks were by Alauddin Khilji in 1303. In fact, he wrested the Kohinoor diamond from the Kakatiya ruler. Later, they were attacked by the Tughlaqs and finally routed by Ghiyasuddin Tughlaq in 1323 in the siege of Warangal. Kakatiya ruler Prataparudra II killed himself as he was taken prisoner, thereby ending the dynasty.

A KAKATIYA SCULPTURE OF LORD VISHNU

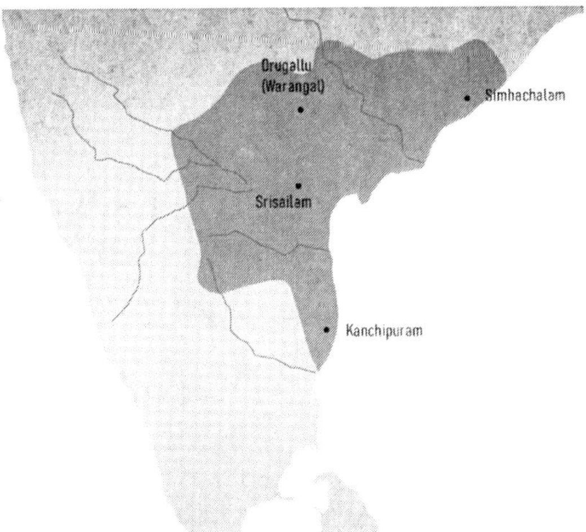

■ THE KAKATIYA TERRITORIES

11 The Zamorins of Calicut

Hereditary monarchs of the kingdom of Calicut on the Malabar Coast of India, the Zamorins ruled for six centuries from the 12th to 16th century CE.

1 The Eradis kingdom, as it was locally known, was established originally by the Hindu vassals of the Later Chera kingdom. During the decline of the Cheras, the Eradis took over the city of Calicut, which they later established as their capital. They were given the title of Samuthiri, or 'Lord of the Seas', anglicized as 'Zamorins'.

AN ARTIST'S IMPRESSION OF THE ZAMORIN OF CALICUT

2 Under the Zamorins, Calicut emerged as a major trading centre of the Eastern world. Trade with the Arabs and the Chinese merchants included pepper, textiles, ginger and cinnamon. Wealth from trade helped them keep a huge army. They maintained relationships across the world. Afanasy Nikitin, the first known Russian to travel to India, and Vasco da Gama, the earliest known Portuguese to come to India, visited Calicut. Ibn Battuta, a Moroccan explorer, and Duarte Barbosa, a Portuguese writer also mentioned the Zamorins.

3 The arrival of Vasco da Gama in Calicut in 1498 marked the control of the oceans passing to the Europeans. Soon, the Dutch landed there in 1604 and the Zamorins allied with them to oust the Portuguese. In 1766, Hyder Ali from Mysore conquered Calicut, ending Zamorin rule.

THE ZAMORIN'S PALACE

12 The Mab'ar Sultanate

Reigning briefly as a small dynasty centred in modern-day Madurai, the Mab'ar dynasty ruled from 1335 to 1378 CE. It was the only Muslim kingdom during its time amidst the several Hindu kingdoms in south India.

1 Despite being a small kingdom and ruling dynasty, the Mab'ar or Madurai Sultanate is noteworthy because its rise can be linked to the Delhi Sultanate, who conquered Tamil Nadu for the first time in this period. An internal quarrel in the Pandya royal family led one of the warring brothers to seek an alliance with Alauddin Khilji of the Delhi Sultanate. Khilji, with no previous plans to invade Tamil Nadu, finally went on to annex the Pandya territory itself. The region then passed on to the corrupt and inefficient Tughlaqs, the next dynasty in the Delhi Sultanate, resulting in a revolt. The governor of Madurai, Jalaluddin Ahsan Khan, declared independence from Delhi and set up the Mab'ar Sultanate in 1335 CE, ruling over a territory that included present-day Madurai, Tiruchirappalli, Cuddalore and Villupuram in Tamil Nadu.

2 The Mab'ar Sultanate left an Islamic cultural legacy in a predominantly Hindu-ruled Tamil Nadu. They introduced elements of Islamic architecture, including arches. They had a well maintained currency system, using the 'copper paisa', featuring Persian inscriptions and art.

3 The famous explorer Ibn Battuta visited the court of Jalaluddin Ahsan Khan and married his daughter. He was impressed with what he saw, but also recorded in the cruelties and discriminatory practices of the sultan. Within two decades, the sultanate started to decline due to infighting and the rise of the Vijayanagara Empire.

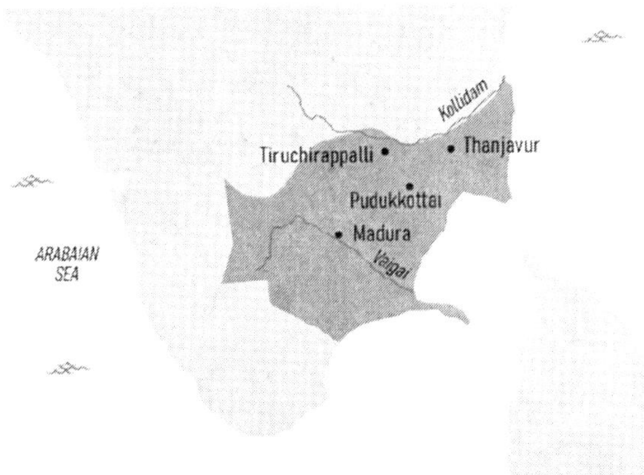

THE MAB'AR SULTANATE

13 The Vijayanagara Empire

Located in the Deccan Plateau of south India, the Vijayanagara Empire was prominent from 1336 to 1646 CE.

1 The Vijayanagara Empire was founded by two brothers, Harihara and Bukka Raya, in the wake of rebellions against the inefficient Tughlaq rulers of the Deccan. It started with the conquest of small sultanates in south India, including the Mab'ar Sultanate, which ruled over a large part of Tamil Nadu. They then went on to take over the Pandya kingdom. The empire got its name from the city of Vijayanagara, in modern-day Hampi, which was their capital. The real golden age of the empire came during the rule of Krishnadevaraya (reign: 1509–29 CE). Creative and performance arts, literature and culture flourished and grand temple-building projects were undertaken. He expanded his empire to the fertile Raichur Doab, between the rivers Krishna and Tungabhadra. A network of canals brought water right into Hampi. He also increased the land revenue, and improved trade with the Portuguese, vastly boosting the economy.

STONE CHARIOT, HAMPI

2 The empire exported perfumes, fabrics, utensils, spices, salt and sugar, and imported China silk, pearls and even horses. It set up embassies in the Ming Empire in China to facilitate trade. They built great temples in the 'Vijayanagara style', with decorative pillars and entrance towers, using granite and soapstone, drawing from the Chalukya, Hoysala, Pandya and Chola styles. Examples include the Chandikeshwara and Uddhana Virabhadra temples in Hampi. They promoted fresco, a wall art using watercolours on wet plaster. Their empire was also known for its great sculptural projects, such as the monolithic Nandi, Lord Shiva's mount, in Hampi.

3 After the death of Krishnadevaraya in 1529, the empire declined, due to weak successors and military rebellions. Rama Raya, the son-in-law of Krishnadevaraya, became the virtual ruler, involving himself in internal fights between the Deccan sultans to boost his power. Eventually, the four Deccan sultans – Ahmednagar, Bijapur, Bidar and Golkonda – formed a victorious alliance against him. He was beheaded and the fragmented empire survived until 1646. Its fall ended the separate political evolutionary paths of south and north India.

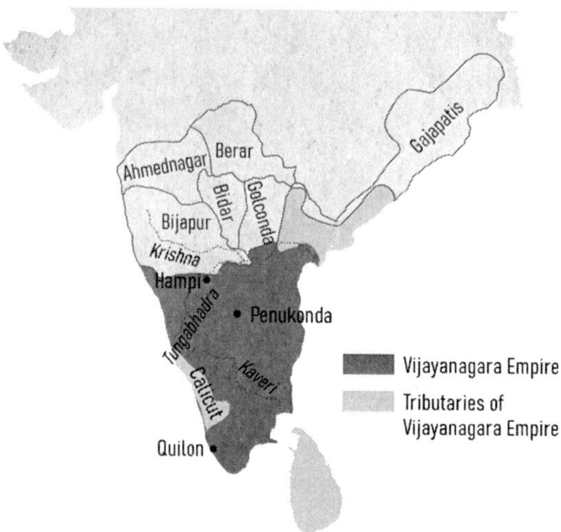

THE VIJAYANAGARA EMPIRE

14 The Mughal Empire

A dynasty of Turkic-Mongol origin that ruled over most of South Asia for over two centuries, the Mughal Empire existed from 1526 to 1857 CE.

1 The Mughal dynasty's name was derived from the Mongols, an East Asian ethnic group native to Mongolia. The dynasty was founded in India by Babur, a descendant of Genghis Khan from his mother's side and of Timur (or Timur the Lame) from his father's side. Babur inherited a small kingdom - Fergana in eastern Uzbekistan - but was ousted by his relatives. Hence, he turned his attention towards Samarkand, another city in Uzbekistan. He conquered it and then made his way towards India. By defeating Ibrahim Lodi of the Delhi Sultanate in the First Battle of Panipat in 1526 CE, he established Mughal rule. Soon after, he began expanding his kingdom by conquering Mewar under Rana Sangha in the Battle of Khanwa. Though briefly, later Humayun, the son of Babur, lost ground to the Afghan ruler Sher Shah Suri. He returned and, in 1555, recaptured the territory earlier under the Mughals.

2 Akbar, the third Mughal ruler, is considered the greatest of all in the dynasty. He expanded his empire into all four cardinal regions of India, thereby controlling the entire subcontinent at one point. He built a strong economy, increased trade, ushered in a modern administrative system and encouraged cultural developments. He practised religious tolerance and even established a new interfaith, syncretic religion, called the Din-i-Ilahi ('divine faith'). During his grandson Shahjahan's reign, the Mughal style of architecture reached its golden age, evinced in the construction of the wondrous Taj Mahal in Agra.

GROUP PORTRAIT OF MUGHAL RULERS

3 Under its next ruler, Aurangzeb, the empire, extending across the whole of South Asia, became one of the most powerful economies in the world. However, Aurangzeb's rule was infamous for its intolerance towards non-Muslims. After his time, the Mughal dynasty began its slow decline. Over a couple of generations that followed, civil wars brewed across the empire. Its regions were

either conquered by formidable enemies, such as the Marathas, or smaller rulers who disassociated themselves to form independent kingdoms.

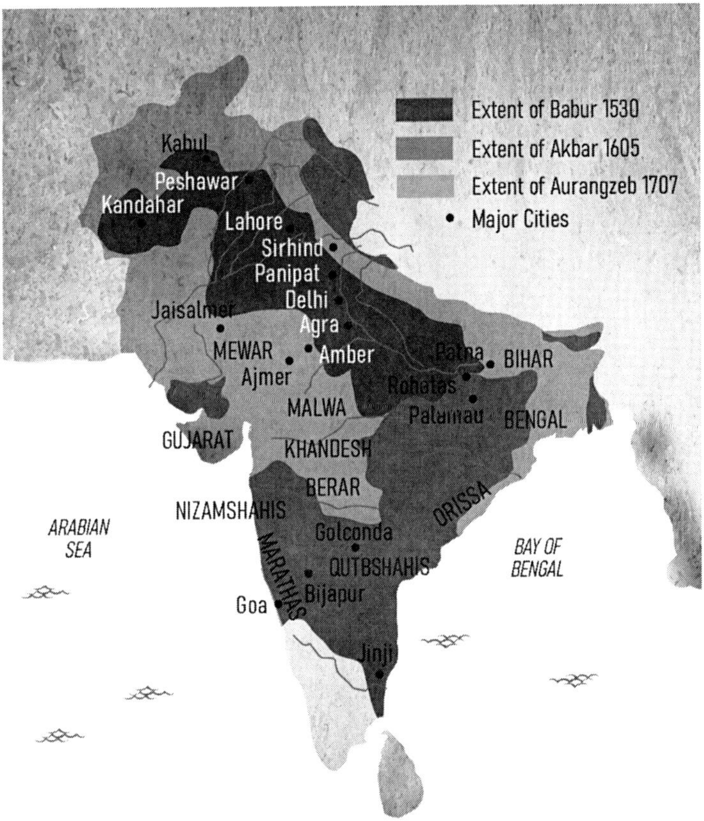

THE MUGHAL EMPIRE

15 The Maratha Empire

Dominating large areas of the Indian subcontinent, the Marathas ruled from 1674 to 1818 CE.

1 A Hindu warrior clan, the Marathas, were settled in the western part of the Deccan Plateau, holding large land settlements. Under their founder, Chhatrapati Shivaji Maharaj, they conquered regions from the Bijapur sultans, creating an independent Maratha kingdom in 1674 CE. He then attacked the territories of the Mughal emperor, Aurangzeb,

CHHATRAPATI SHIVAJI MAHARAJ

and expanded the empire towards the south, south-east and north. He also built a formidable navy with battleships and several sea forts (*jala durg*).

MARATHA NAVY ATTACKING AN ENGLISH SHIP

2 In 1689, Shivaji's son Sambhaji was executed by Mughal forces, and the Marathas saw a short period of decline. However, in 1713, the tide turned with the Peshwa line of Marathas. In 1719, they marched to Delhi after conquering the Mughal governor of the Deccan. In 1728, they defeated the kingdom under the Nizam of Hyderabad. Their armies also overran present-day Odisha and West Bengal, and pushed towards north-western India, defeating the Durrani Empire, who retaliated in 1761 with local allies, defeating the Marathas in the Third Battle of Panipat, thereby halting their expansion. While in power, the Maratha administration set up better systems of revenue collection and new trade networks, made agriculture and banking more efficient and encouraged art and culture. They promoted both Sanskrit and Marathi literature, and the grand tradition of textile weaving, including Paithani saris woven in silk and gold.

3 After the Third Battle of Panipat, the empire was fragmented. The British meddled in Maratha kingdom, leading to three Anglo-Maratha Wars. By the third war (1817–18), the Peshwas were exiled and the British gained control.

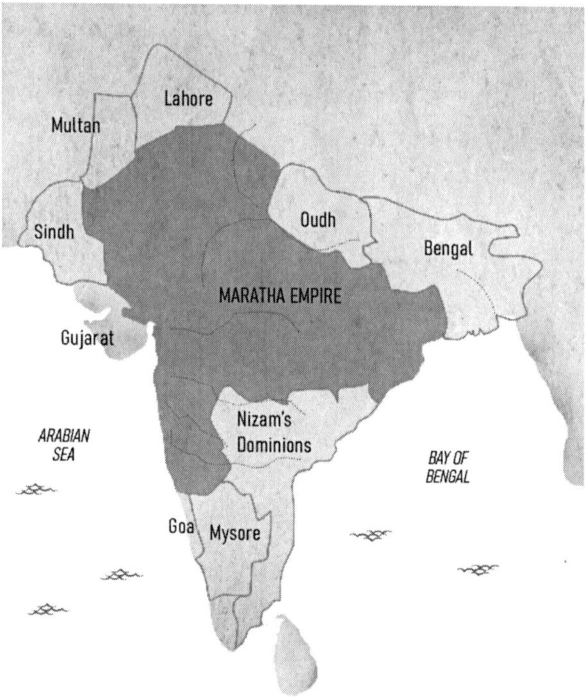

■ THE MARATHA EMPIRE (1758)

SOUTH-EAST ASIAN AND CHINESE EMPIRES

16 The Srivijaya Empire

A kingdom founded near the sea, the Srivijaya Empire was based largely in Indonesia and spilled over to the Malay Archipelago. It ruled over these parts from the seventh to the 13th century CE.

1 The Srivijaya Empire was founded by Emperor Dapunta Hyang Sri Jayanasa in Palembang, in Indonesia, during the eighth century CE. His kingdom expanded into Java and the Malay Peninsula, controlling important trade routes in the region. Unlike most empires that looked at conquests for territorial expansion, the Srivijaya empire depended mostly on trade to make inroads.

2 The empire controlled two major passageways in the trade between the wealthy regions of India and China: the Strait of Malacca and the Sunda Strait. Their main trading partners were the Cholas from India, with whom they traded in ivory, tin, sandalwood and spices. From China they procured silk and porcelain. With the wealth accumulated from trade, the empire propagated Buddhism, becoming an important centre for

Buddhist learning, especially of the Vajrayana sect. The region attracted pilgrims and scholars from across the world. They even set up many Buddhist monasteries in Nagapattinam in south India.

3 The empire's decline began when the Cholas under Rajendra Chola attacked them in a series of naval raids in 1025 CE, tipping the balance of power in maritime trade. The Singosari Empire of East Java absorbed the empire in 1288 CE. However, the impact of Srivijaya endured, as the trade routes they established remain strategic for world trade even now.

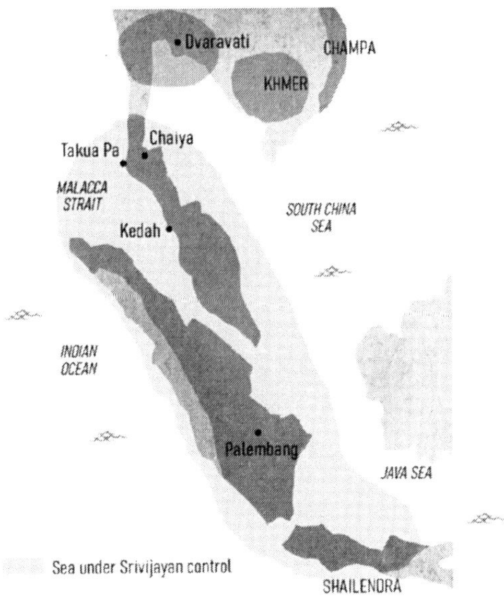

THE SRIVIJAYA EMPIRE

17 The Shailendra Kingdom

A maritime dynasty that flourished in South-East Asia, the Shailendra kingdom was based in Java from about 750 to 850 CE.

1 It is unknown how the kingdom was established, but historians posit that the promotion of Buddhism by empires such as the Srivijaya kingdom contributed to the rise of the Shailendra kingdom. It started its main military expansions under Emperor Sri Kesari Warmadewa, with the intent

BOROBUDUR TEMPLE COMPLEX

to promote Buddhism. He led multiple successful military campaigns and expeditions, one such being into Bali, Indonesia, to establish a Buddhist government. The Blanjong pillar with inscriptions in Sanur in Bali is dedicated to this effort.

2 The strategic location of Java in trade – midway between India (from where spices, gold, jewels and pearls made their way) and China (from where goods such as silk, tea and porcelain came) – helped the Shailendras to gain prominence. They maintained trading relationships with the Champa kingdom of South-East Asia and the Cholas of south India. The Shailendras also undertook agricultural ventures, such as rice cultivation, spread across central Java, an area with fertile volcanic soil. The kingdom was also well known for its propagation of Buddhism around the world. Together with the Srivijaya Empire, they ushered in a golden age for Buddhism. Despite being religiously inclined, they coexisted peacefully with another great kingdom in central Java, the Sanjaya dynasty, a Hindu kingdom. They were also known for their art and architecture, commissioning beautiful sculptures and inscriptions. Between 778 and 824 CE, they constructed the Borobudur Temple complex, a renowned Buddhist monument,

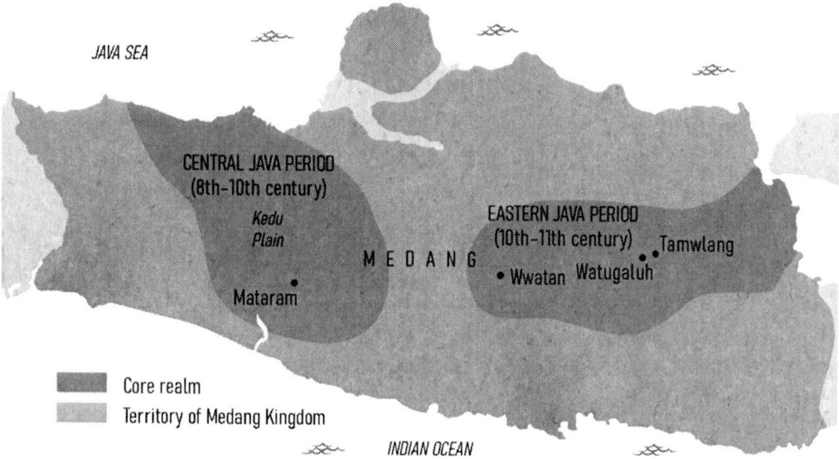

THE SHAILENDRA EMPIRE

along with other temples, such as Candi Mendut, Candi Kalsan and Candi Sewu in Java, Indonesia.

3 There's no consensus amongst historians on the decline of the Shailendra kingdom. Some say it was conquered by the Sanjaya dynasty, while others say they were invaded by the Cholas. There is also a theory that the Shailendra kingdom merged with the Srivijaya kingdom through intermarriages. The Shailendras gave South-East Asia its first large-scale Buddhist monument – the massive stupa of Borobudur.

18 The Khmer Empire

Located in South-East Asia, the Khmer Empire had much of Cambodia, Thailand and Vietnam under its control. It existed from 790 CE to the 15th century CE. The empire referred to itself as Kambuja, the early name for Cambodia.

1 A young prince, Jayavarman II, broke away from the Srivijaya Empire to establish the Khmer kingdom in eastern Cambodia. Over the next decade, the empire extended towards the Mekong river valley. Their capital was in Angkor and they fought many wars with their rivals, the Srivijaya Empire.

2 The Khmer Empire had a planned economy-based trade of rice and fish. Almost 80 per cent of the population was involved in growing rice. As the empire bordered the River Mekong, it helped them develop fishing as a revenue source. They established several trade ports and trade partnerships with south India. The empire was known for its rich culture displayed in its architectural pursuits. Ahead of its time and urbanized, it boasted modern features, such as an

elaborate road system and a vast canal network. But its greatest contribution was the construction of the 200-hectare Angkor Wat complex, a UNESCO World Heritage Site since 1992. Built by king Suryavarman II around 1122 CE, it was initially built to be a Buddhist monastery, though it later housed many Hindu deities.

3 The empire's decline could have been the result of overspending on lavish construction projects, or due to a series of natural disasters. The rise of rival powers in Vietnam and Thailand, including the Ayutthaya kingdom, could have accentuated this process.

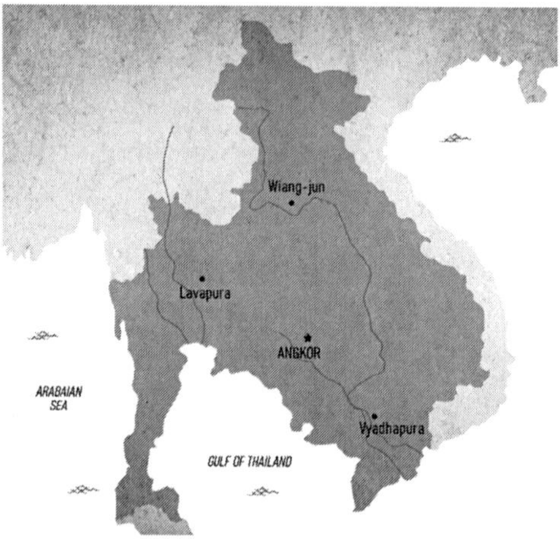

■ THE KHMER EMPIRE

19 The Ayutthaya Kingdom

A Siamese kingdom, ruling from 1350 to 1767 CE, the Ayutthaya kingdom existed in the northern part of present-day Bangkok.

1 It started out as a small kingdom, one among the several warring states in Thailand. Little is known of its founding king, Ramathibodi. His kingdom bordered the powerful Khmer Empire. Eventually, Ayutthaya power grew and they overran Khmer and took over their capital of Angkor in 1431 CE. During King Narai's rule, trade routes were extended and the kingdom expanded. By the end of the 14th century CE, the Ayutthaya regime was one of the strongest powers in South-East Asia.

AN AYUTTHAYA KING

2 The Ayyuthaya Empire cultivated extensive trading relationships with China, South-East Asia and India. They also propagated Buddhism by establishing missions in Sri Lanka and even in Europe. In 1350 CE, they founded the

city of Ayutthaya, which grew into one of the most cosmopolitan and urban cities in the world. The kingdom also led massive construction projects thanks to the abundance of construction materials, such as bricks, stucco and bronze. It established several great Buddhist temples, built in pyramid or square shapes, their interiors decorated with murals and sculptures – some examples are the Wat Mahathat, Wat Phra Si Sanphet and Wat Yai Chai Mongkhon in Thailand. Sculpture-making flourished, the most famous one depicting the Buddha peeping out of a banyan tree in Wat Mahathat.

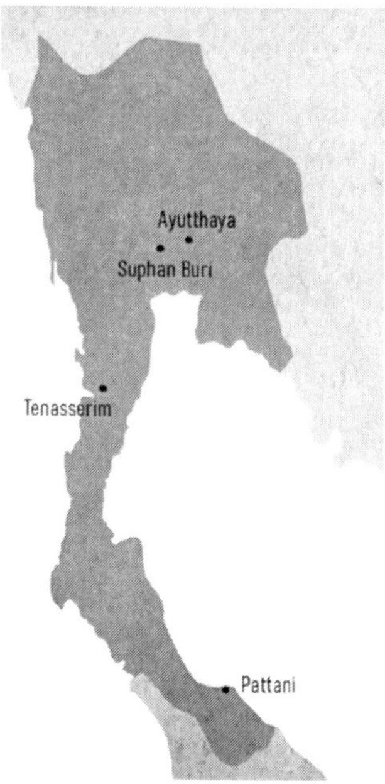

THE AYUTTHAYA KINGDOM

3 The Ayutthaya kingdom saw a decline due to attacks from neighbouring Burmese kingdoms. Despite being overrun by a Burmese kingdom in 1569 CE, they recovered. However, the threat persisted and, in 1767 CE, the city of Ayutthaya was captured, leading to the collapse of the ruling dynasty.

20 The Toungoo Empire

A dominant empire and power in South-East Asia, the Toungoo regime was centred mainly in Myanmar. It existed from 1510 to 1752 CE.

1 The Toungoo Empire was initially a small vassal state in the Ava Kingdom in Burma. It started its expansion in the 1530s, under King Tabinshwehti, who initially conquered petty states in Myanmar before setting out for larger conquests. By the time of his death in 1550, Toungoo emerged as one of the largest empires in South-East Asia and included regions like present-day Manipur in India, and the Chinese Shan territories, Siam and Lan Xang. From 1510 to 1599 CE, the empire saw an internal rebellion aided by rivals and Portuguese mercenaries, followed by a reunification, which restored Toungoo authority in Upper Burma and the Shan territories by 1606 CE, before declining by the mid-1700s.

2 The kings Mingyi Nyo, Tabinshwehti, Bayinnaung and Nanda Bayin reigned over the empire at its peak, enabling it to rival even China in terms of dominance. Under its greatest

rulers, the empire expanded, not only militarily, but also culturally, politically and economically. A well-organized currency system was introduced. The empire also promoted art and architecture, such as beautiful teakwood idols and copper statues of its emperors, including one of King Bayinnaung. Their paintings were intricate and featured creatures they considered sacred, such as elephants or peacocks.

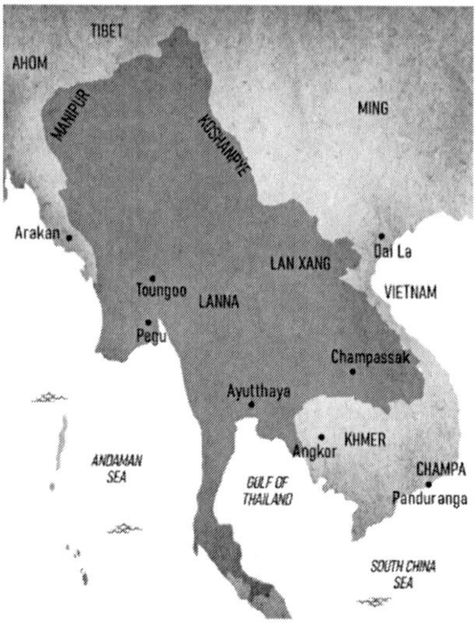

■ TOUNGOO TERRITORIES

3 The dynasty declined in the 18th century, due to institutional weaknesses, factionalism, succession disputes and internal rebellions instigated by many European powers, including the French. However, it is credited for uniting several independent kingdoms in Myanmar under a single banner for a sustained period of time.

21 The Tang Empire

One of the most powerful regimes in the imperial history of China, the Tang Empire ushered in a golden age of Chinese arts and culture. It lasted from 618 to 907 CE.

1 After the fall of the Han dynasty in 220 CE, China went through a period of quick dynastic successions until the Sui dynasty, which ruled from 589 to 618 CE. They united north and south China, and streamlined the bureaucracy. During the final years of the Sui dynasty, the empire was deep in debt, resulting in a rebellion led by Li Yuan, a military commander turned rebel, which culminated in the assassination of the Sui emperor. Li Yuan took the throne as Emperor Gaozu, in 618 CE, founding the Tang dynasty.

2 Emperor Gaozu reformed the bureaucratic and taxation regime, created the Tang legal code and redistributed land to common peasants. He was followed by Taizong, regarded as the co-founder of the dynasty along with his father. He built on his father's progressive initiatives, and

followed a policy of religious tolerance and further improvements in governance and military. During the period of the third emperor, Emperor Gaozong, the empire saw the rise of Empress Wu, who took over the empire and started controlling the imperial administration. Empress Wu was China's only woman ruler, and she brought in widespread reforms in agriculture, taxation, education and administration. The seventh ruler, Emperor Xuanzong who ruled for 44 years from 712 CE, ushered in a golden age in China. Buddhism was elevated as the most popular religion but Taoism was also promoted. The economy improved multifold, owing to financial reforms, increased trade and improved infrastructure networks. Border and homeland security stabilized. Art, literature and architecture flourished, where over 50,000 poems and plays and an encyclopedia were produced during this period. Medicine, science and technology progressed, and many innovations were made, including gunpowder, waterproofing, the introduction of the gas stove, fireproofing and even air conditioning!

EMPRESS WU AND EMPEROR XUANZONG

3 By the end of Xuanzong's rule, growth tapered, followed by a series of weak rulers. There were revolts, accentuated by widespread famines, droughts and food shortages. In 907 CE, the last Tang emperor, Ai, was assassinated by a Chinese general Zhu Wen, resulting in the end of the empire. This was followed by the 'Five Dynasties' and 'Ten Kingdoms' period from 907 to 979 CE, with many short-lived regimes and political upheavals until the founding of the Song dynasty in 960 CE.

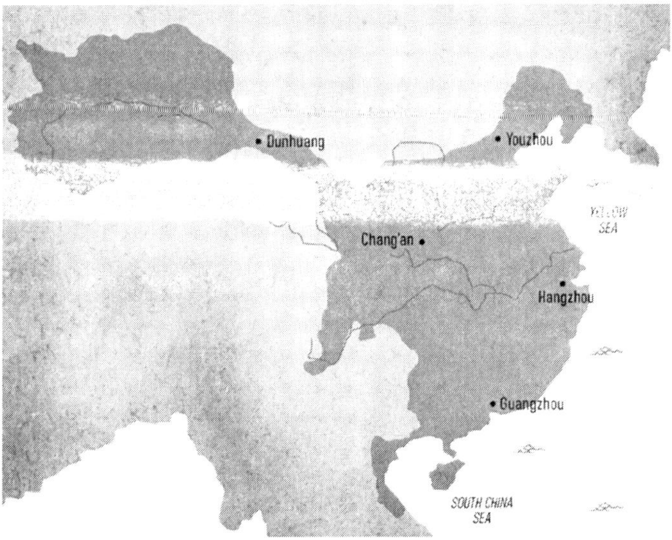

THE TANG EMPIRE, 700 CE

22 The Qing Dynasty

Also known as the Manchu dynasty, the Qing dynasty was the final imperial dynasty of China. It ruled from 1644 to 1912 CE.

1 In 1640, the Ming dynasty in China began to decline as it faced a tremendous financial crisis accentuated by natural disasters. Civil wars and peasant uprisings broke out across the empire, including one led by a Ming general, Li Zicheng, who eventually overthrew the weakened empire. The Manchus of Manchuria, an ethnic minority in China, Li Zicheng's allies in this rebellion, took advantage of this crisis, installed their emperor on the throne of China and founded the Qing dynasty. The Qings ensured that the Manchus controlled the administration against the majority Hans, by allocating higher and more powerful bureaucratic positions to their kith and kin.

2 The second emperor, Kangxi, took the throne in 1654 CE and ruled for 61 years, the longest for any Chinese emperor. During his reign, the dynasty reached its pinnacle. This period was

known as the High Qing era. The empire expanded towards Russia, extended across Outer Mongolia, and into Tibet and Nepal. They also successfully crushed Han rebellions and defeated the Mongols. The local administration stabilized, taxes were reduced and corruption brought under control. Confucius's teachings were reinstated and a neo-Confucian culture flourished. The Qings leveraged the Silk Route and monopolized the worldwide demand for tea during the time.

THE KANGXI EMPEROR

3 During the mid-1800s, China, under the Qings, faced several challenges, including a burgeoning population, famine, floods and food shortages. As the Manchu armies were considerably weakened during this time, there were several rebellions. All efforts to modernize China were met with severe opposition from the conservative, bureaucratic officials, who were inefficient and steeped in corruption. The Opium Wars against Britain and France, the Sino-Japanese war and the Boxer Rebellion, all resulted in losses and China's defeat. The failing regime was then challenged by

a revolution led by political leader Sun Yat-Sen, resulting in the abdication of the throne and the establishment of the Provisional Government of the Republic of China, in which Sun Yat-sen was elected as the provincial president on 1 January 1912.

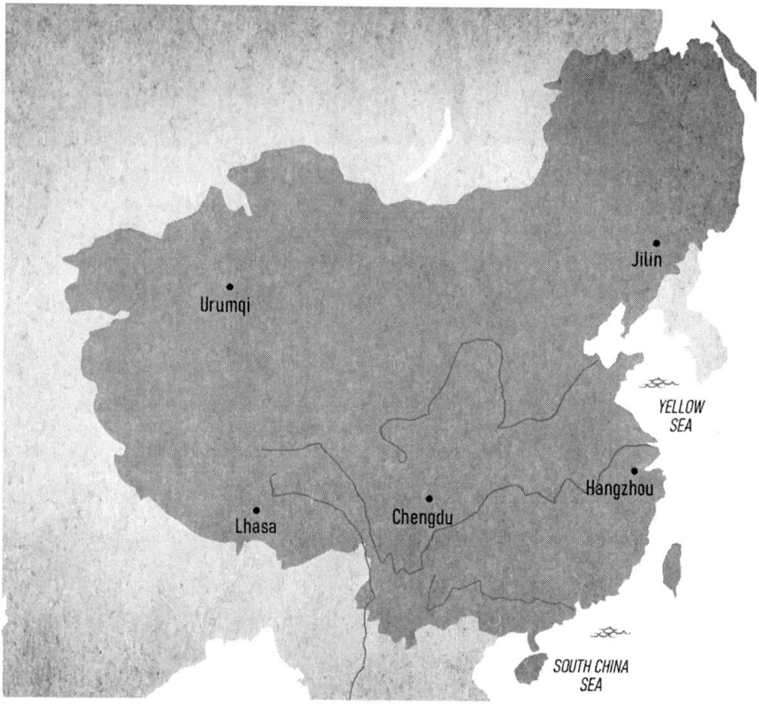

THE QING EMPIRE

PERSIAN EMPIRES AND MONGOL KHANATES

23 The Umayyad Caliphate

The second of the four major caliphates, the Umayyad Caliphate is believed to have descended from the Prophet Muhammad. It existed from 661 to 750 CE.

1 The assassination of Ali, the son-in-law of Prophet Muhammad, was a major defining moment for early Muslims. During this time, Ali's governor of Syria, Muawiyah, who was a descendant of the Quraysh tribe in Mecca, emerged as the sole ruler of the Muslim world. But a civil war followed, called the First Fitna, and Muawiyah overthrew the previous Rashidun Caliphate and established the Umayyad Caliphate in 661 CE. He expanded his empire across the Middle East and established Damascus as his capital. The early period of the Umayyad dynasty, when Muawiyah ruled, is known as the Sufyanid period, lasting from 661 to 684 CE. It was followed by the Marwanid period from 684 to 750 CE.

2 Moving the Umayyad Caliphate capital from Mecca to Syria enabled them to use the Syrian army as their base to build a centralized

Islamic state. The Umayyad Empire spread from Sidh in north-west Africa to the Iberian Peninsula, making it one of the largest empires in the world in terms of area. Arabic was adopted as their national language, the financial administration was reorganized and a uniform system of coinage was established. A postal service was introduced to improve communication between Damascus and the other regions of the empire. Architecture flourished, and marvels such as the Dome of Rock in Jerusalem, and next to it the Al-Aqsa Mosque, the third holiest mosque in the Islamic world, were built during this time. The caliphate also improved trade relations across the vast swathes of lands they occupied.

AL-AQSA MOSQUE

3 The decline of the Umayyad dynasty started with their defeat by the Byzantine Empire in 717 CE. This led to a financial crisis, resulting in a civil war that weakened their military strength. In 749 CE, one of the revolting religious factions challenged the legitimacy of Umayyad rule, with their leader proclaiming himself as the new caliph, thereby establishing the Abbasid dynasty.

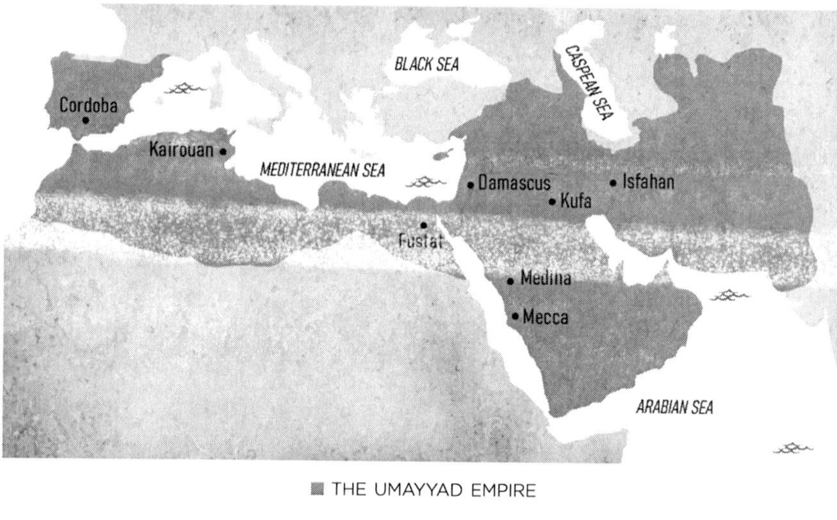

THE UMAYYAD EMPIRE

24 The Abbasid Caliphate

Counted amongst the four main caliphates in history, the Abbasid Caliphate called themselves the descendants of Abbas ibn Abd al-Muttalib, a merchant and a follower of Prophet Muhammad. The caliphate existed from 750 to 1258 CE.

1 In 750 CE, the Abbasids invaded the Umayyad Caliphate that extended through North Africa and the Strait of Gibraltar, and included the Iberian Peninsula. This helped them to establish themselves as a major power in Asia that extended throughout the Middle East and Egypt. The Abbasid rulers, or caliphs, established a flourishing trade network along this vast kingdom. Trade in soaps, ivory, honey and diamonds fuelled the economy. They appointed officials called 'viziers' to help govern the kingdom.

2 The Abbasid Caliphate's rule ushered in an Islamic golden age, promoting culture and arts alongside commerce and industry. In Baghdad, the caliphate established the 'House of Wisdom' or the Grand Library, visited by scholars from around the world. The Abbasids had texts from

around the world translated into Arabic, including many important Hindu Sanskrit scriptures. Many great Arab thinkers, such as Al-Farabi, Al- Khwarizmi and Omar Khayyam, gained prominence in history, philosophy and astronomy.

ABBASID ENVOYS PRESENTING A WATER CLOCK TO CHARLEMAGNE

3 In 1258, the Mongol Empire, under Hulagu Khan, invaded the Abbasid Empire. The Mongols pillaged and burnt the House of Wisdom, and this incident sparked the end of the Abbasid Caliphate.

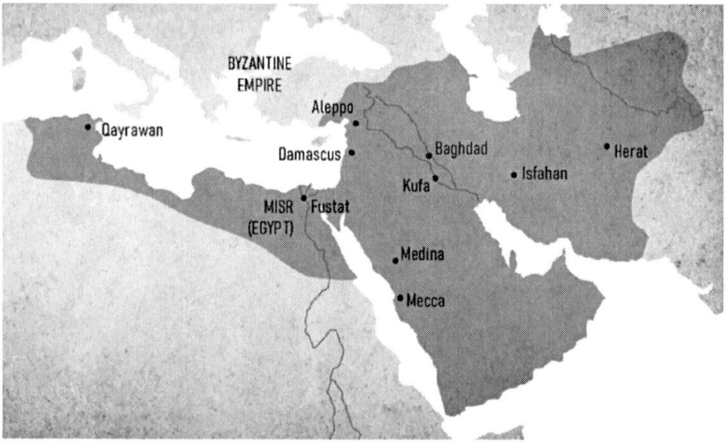

ABBASID CALIPHATE TERRITORIES

25 The Seljuk Empire

A Turkic-Persian Muslim empire, The Seljuk Empire was founded in 999 CE and lasted until 1230 CE.

1 The Seljuk dynasty was founded by Seljuk, a warlord from a Turkic state called Oghuz Yabgu. He migrated, along with his tribe, to Khwarezm, a region belonging to present-day Turkmenistan; it is here that they converted to Islam. Khwarezm, during those days, was under the Samanids, an Islamic Persian empire. When this region was attacked, the Seljuks strategically supported the Samanids, which allowed them eventually to establish their own independent kingdom.

2 The Seljuk Empire started expanding after being taken over by the grandsons of Seljuk - Chagri and Tughril. They ventured into Iran, lower central Asia and Mesopotamia, winning some territories through alliances and many through conquests. Chagri's son further extended the kingdom into Armenia, Georgia and to Anatolia from the Byzantine Empire in 1068. In the later years, the Seljuk Empire's frontiers bordered China

in the east and the Byzantine Empire in the west. Islam went alongside the Seljuks' expansionist projects. A network of Islam-centric colleges was founded, bureaucrats were trained in Islamic studies and large architectural projects, including the Great Mosque of Esfahan in Iran, were built. Owing to this, the Seljuks came to be regarded as the restorers of Islamic unity, which allowed them to play a key role in the First and Second Crusades.

3 In 1092, the empire was split up due to internal feuds over succession. On the Anatolian part was later founded the Sultanate of

THE GREAT MOSQUE OF ISFAHAN

Rum, a branch of the Seljuks, based in modern Turkey, established over the conquered Byzantine territories. Eventually, in 1230 CE, a war instigated by the Rum sultan against the Khwarezm-Shah dynasty of Persia resulted in the former's defeat and the disintegration of the Seljuk Empire. Their territories were then taken over by the Mongols.

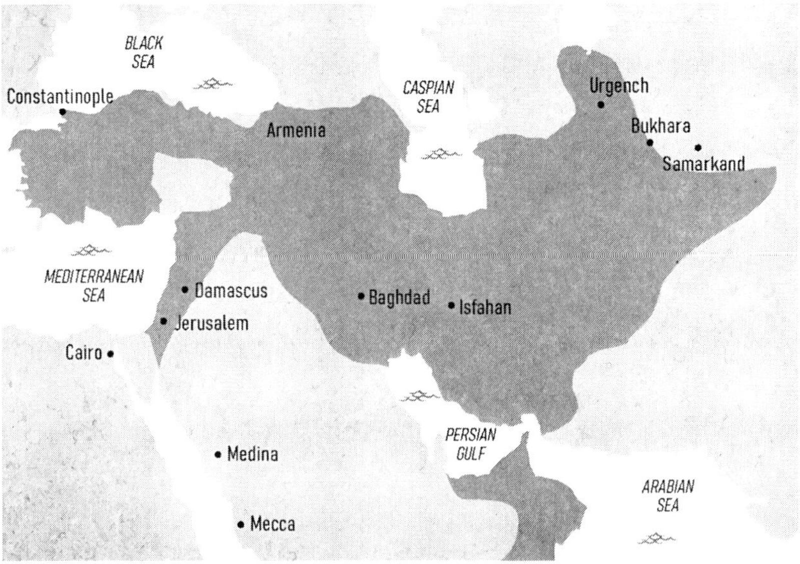

THE SELJUK SULTANATE

26 The Ottoman Empire

A Eurasian empire that dominated Turkey, the Ottoman Empire grew to be one of the most powerful empires in the world. It existed from 1299 to 1922 CE.

1 According to historical records of the Ottomans, the empire originated from the Kayi tribe branch of the Oghuz Turks, one of the many Turkish states that started rising by the end of the 13th century CE. After the fall of the Seljuk Empire, the Turkic-Persian Muslim empire, Osman Bey, one of their chieftains attacked and conquered the fortresses of Kuluca Hisar, now in Turkey, in a battle that he fought against the Byzantine Empire. Osman continued his winning streak by conquering Yenisehir, Turkey which would later become the capital of the Ottoman Empire, a dynasty that he founded as Osman I.

EMPEROR MEHMET II

2 After Osman, his son Orhan ascended the throne and expanded the empire across the Eastern Roman Empire territories in Anatolia and Europe, even taking over the Balkans. He used his conquests to establish a sophisticated military organization method called the Janissaries - Christian soldiers taken in as war slaves, converted to Islam and given positions in the Ottoman army. Orhan also introduced the *jizya*, a tax levied on all non-Muslims, enabling the Ottomans to fund further military expansion. In 1402, the Ottoman Sultan Bayezid I was defeated by Timur, but the sultan's son Mehmet I returned to power in the Battle of Ankara. However, the definitive victory for the Ottomans came with Mehmet II's conquest of Constantinople, the pride of the Byzantine Empire, in 1453 CE. After this, they expanded their empire towards both east and west, including the regions of the Black Sea, Persia and Egypt. The Ottoman Sultans took the title of Caliph, as the holy cities of Mecca, Medina and Jerusalem came under them.

3 By the end of the 1600s, the Ottoman Empire's power started to decline, and they were forced to give up large European territories. They were also affected by civil wars and revolutions across their empire, including the Greek Revolution,

followed by several regions breaking away. Many European imperialist regimes, like Britain, Italy and France, started to rise and dominate Ottoman territories under the guise of trade. The empire was wiped out in 1922 once they decided to ally with the losing Central Powers in the First World War. The Turkish War of Independence, fought from 1919 to 1923 CE, led by military leader and statesman Mustafa Kemal Ataturk, brought a formal end to the empire.

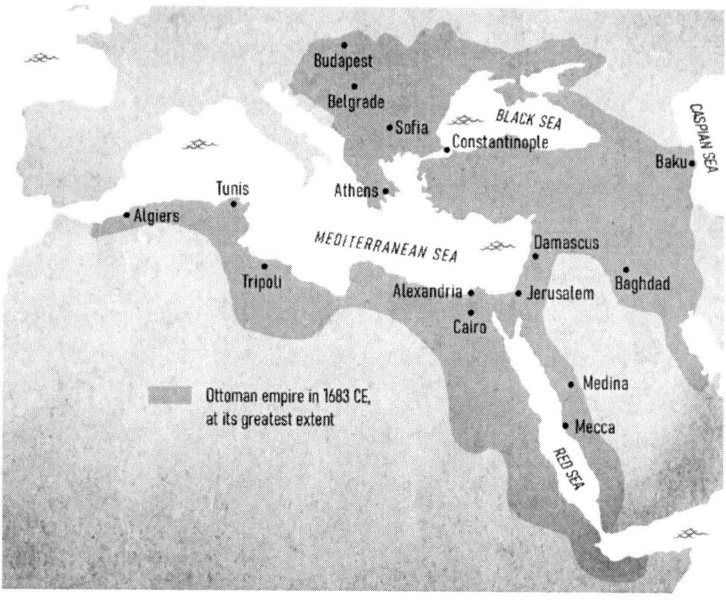

THE OTTOMAN EMPIRE

27 The Mongol Empire

The largest contiguous land empire recorded in history and also the second largest empire in terms of land mass, after the British Empire, the Mongol Empire existed from 1206 to 1368 CE.

1 The Mongol Empire was established by Genghis Khan, born in 1162. Until then, the East Asian steppe had many warring nomadic tribes. By 1206, Genghis conquered and unified the Mongols, Keraites, Tatars, Uyghurs and other small tribes, under one name, the Mongols, and one ruler 'the Great Khan'. He was supported by his able military leaders, such Subotai the Valiant, who won 65 pre-planned battles. Genghis's unconventional strategies of absorbing conquered soldiers, scattering them across his army to prevent rebel uprisings, and promoting them based on skill and not lineage, helped him expand his empire at a faster pace.

2 In 1227, Genghis died during a campaign against the Chinese Xi Xia kingdom. The Mongol Empire was then taken over by Genghis's third son, Ogedei, as the next Great Khan

while regencies of various regions were allocated to the other heirs. Ogedei Khan added present-day Iran and many parts of Europe, including Georgia and Armenia, to the empire. He also invaded present-day Korea, Hungary, Poland, Bulgaria, Croatia, Serbia, Austria and even India under the Delhi Sultanate. In 1259, a succession battle known as the Toluid civil war broke out, between Kublai Khan, one of Genghis's grandsons, and his younger brother, Ariq Boke, resulting in a permanent division of the empire. Kublai Khan eventually took over China and founded the Yuan dynasty. Persia was taken over by the Ilkhanate, while in Asia, the Chagatai Khanate ruled, bringing forth military leaders like Timur the Lame. Timur's descendant Babur later invaded India to found the Mughal Empire. In Eastern Europe, the Kipchak (Ulus of Jochi or Golden Horde), continued their rule. These four parts of the empire were known as the four khanates.

GENGHIS KHAN (TOP) AND OGEDEI KHAN

3 In these khanates, women were given importance and administrative positions, such as Queen Boraqin and Genghis's wife Borte Ujin. The rulers learned to collaborate over the vast territories, resulting in a period of development and relative stability called the Pax Mongolica. However, the khanates started to disintegrate during the mid-1300 CE due to civil wars and weak rulers. The Black Death may have also played an important role, as many khans had previously succumbed to it.

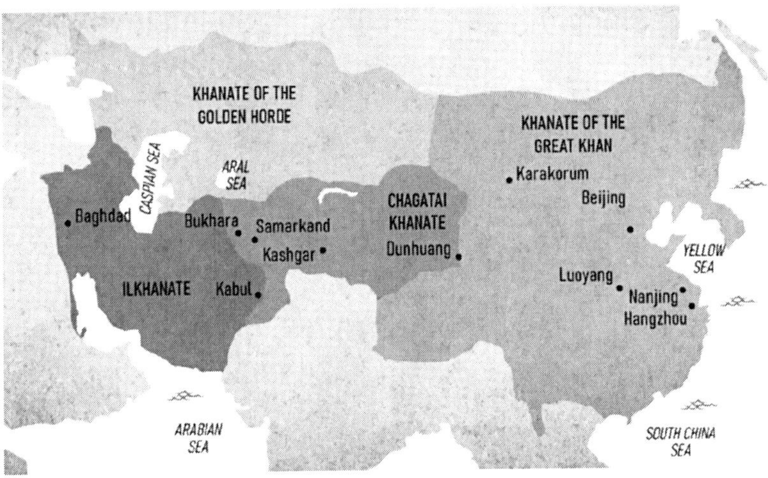

THE MONGOL EMPIRE AND KHANATES

28 The Chagatai Khanate

Part of the Mongol Empire, the Chagatai Khanate covered parts of Uzbekistan, Kazakhstan and Tajikistan. It flourished from 1227 to 1363 CE.

1 When Genghis Khan died in 1227 CE, his second son, Chagatai Khan, inherited the eastern territories of the Khwarazm Empire, a region conquered by Genghis Khan in 1220 CE to avenge the killing of Mongol merchants. However, compared to the other Khanates, which were rich in resources

CHAGATAI PRINCES

and had stable governance, the Chagatai Khanate comprised steppe land inhabited by nomadic tribes with weak institutions and sparse resources. Hence, it remained nomadic in nature, and developed less in economic and cultural terms.

2 Samarkand was established as the capital of the khanate. Chagatai Khan was constantly at war with the other khanates: Kipchak in the north, Ilkhanate in the west and Yuan in the east. From 1290 onwards, the Chagatais began expanding and conquered east Afghanistan. Though they tried to invade India, they were defeated by the Delhi Sultanate. Despite spare resources, the Chagatais were able to collect abundant taxes given that the Silk Road passed through their territories. However, this also meant that they overexploited this source of revenue, ultimately leading to decline in trade.

3 The khanate was fatally weakened due to constant battles, internal power conflicts and frequent change of leaders. This was worsened by the Black Death, which devastated the economy. After the last khan, Tughlugh Timur, the empire disintegrated in 1363 CE. From 1370 CE onwards, the Chagatai Khanate was taken over by Timur the Lame, the founder of the Timurid Empire.

29 The Kipchak Khanate

Also called the Golden Horde, the Kipchak Khanate comprised the western part of the Mongol Empire. It flourished from 1227 to 1380 CE.

1 As the Mongol Empire was divided among the four sons of Genghis Khan, in 1227 CE his first son Jochi received the part around the Ural Mountains and beyond. Jochi's son Batu Khan established the Kipchak Khanate, as he consolidated his empire, starting with the sacking of the city

KIPCHAK WARRIORS

of Kiev in 1240 CE. At the zenith of his conquests, the Kipchak territories extended from Siberia to the Caucasus to Hungary to Constantinople. It encompassed parts of Central Asia, Russia and Eastern Europe, and bordered the Persian territories of the Ilkhanate Empire, another khanate.

2 For the European part of the Mongol Empire, the Kipchaks, it was a period of peace and prosperity known as the Pax Mongolica. Trade flourished because they had the other Mongol empires, including the Yuan and the Ilkhanate, surrounding them. They also had extensive trade relations with their allies, the Mamluks in Egypt. At its peak, this khanate had more than half a million inhabitants. Compared to other parts of the Eastern Europe, the citizens of Kipchak Khanate were safer and more secure.

3 However, like the Ilkhans, the Black Death that struck in 1346, ravaged the Kipchaks. Added to this, there were several civil wars that weakened the empire. In the Battle of Kulikovo in 1380, the Russians defeated the Mongols. Though the Kipchaks were able to retaliate, their empire had seriously weakened, and soon disintegrated.

30 The Ilkhanate Empire

A khanate that ruled over most of modern-day Iran, the Ilkhanate Empire existed from 1256 to 1335 CE.

1 The Ilkhanate Empire was founded when the emperor of Persia, Muhammad II of Khwarazm, assassinated a group of merchants dispatched by the Mongols. The Mongol emperor, Genghis Khan, who had conquered almost all of Asia by then, declared war on the Khwarazm Shah dynasty. Genghis invaded and pillaged Persia.

HULAGU KHAN AND DOKUZ KHATUN

After his death, his sons and grandsons divided among themselves all the land that Genghis had conquered; Persia was given to Hulagu Khan, one of Genghis's grandsons. Hulagu named this territory the Ilkhanate Empire. The other branches of Genghis's empire were the Chagatai Khanate, the Golden Horde and the Yuan Empire.

2 The descendants of Hulagu, called the House of Hulagu, then ruled the Ilkhanate Empire. During the next several decades, the empire expanded across Central Asia and included present-day Iran, Azerbaijan and Turkey. This large-scale conquest kept the flow of culture, wealth and power in the Ilkhanate Empire. Compared to the other branches like the Yuans, the Ilkhans were broadminded. They ruled through a partnership with the local Persian administration, whose members sometimes were not even Muslims or from traditional families. The empire also helped improve trade and commerce across the Asian region. It was known as the golden age for visual arts: Persian miniature painting scaled new heights and architecture flourished. One of the most recognizable styles of building, comprising blue domes as roofs, a hallmark of Persian architecture, evolved during this time. The

AN ILKHAN HORSE-WARRIOR

Ilkhans also encouraged Iranians to move from Arabic writing to native Persian.

3 In 1335, the Ikhanate Empire was ravaged by the bubonic plague, known as the Black Death. With the death of the successor to the throne, a series of internal squabbles followed, resulting in political instability. The Ilkhanate Empire disintegrated rapidly, breaking up into several small khanates. However, in the late 14th century, these smaller khanates were taken over by Timur the Lame, the founder of the Timurid Empire.

31 The Yuan Dynasty

A part of the Mongol Khanate, the Yuan dynasty based in China, ruled from 1271 to 1368 CE. It was established by Kublai Khan, the grandson of the famed Mongol conqueror Genghis Khan.

1 Genghis Khan's campaign in China began with his conquest of western Xia, just after his coronation in 1206 CE. Though he kept at it, the Jin dynasty prevailed. After Genghis died in 1227, the Mongols continued their fight for the Jin region.

YUAN EMPEROR KUBLAI KHAN

More than two decades later, Kublai Khan, one of Genghis's grandsons, allied with the southern Song dynasty to attack the northern Jin dynasty. Later, he turned against the Song and added this region to his empire. Kublai then established his own Chinese dynasty in 1271 CE, the Yuan, and expanded into Mongolia, Russia and other parts of China.

2 With its takeover of China, the Yuan dynasty brought forward several changes. The capital was moved from Karakorum, in Mongolia, to Beijing. They established a centralized bureaucracy, with provincial governments, and made the taxation system more efficient. New roads, canals and postal stations were built to ensure smooth communication within the vast empire and police forces stationed to maintain law and order. Merchants were given a favourable tax regime, low-cost loans were offered and people were encouraged to use paper money. Artists and craftsmen were given several privileges. During Kublai Khan's reign, foreigners were encouraged to visit the empire, a great example being the Venetian explorer Marco Polo. His records on the empire helped to spread word of the Yuan dynasty's power and riches across the world. This helped the dynasty develop a vast trade network. However, the Yuans were not free of discrimination,

favouring Mongols over the local Chinese. Civil service examinations were abolished, and Mongols occupied all positions of power.

3 Kublai Khan was succeeded by his grandson Temur Oljeitu, trailed by a long line of short-term rulers. Civil and succession wars and weak administration led to famines, plagues and floods that devastated the empire, worsened by banditry and civil uprisings. One such rebellion was the Red Turban Movement, led by a Buddhist monk

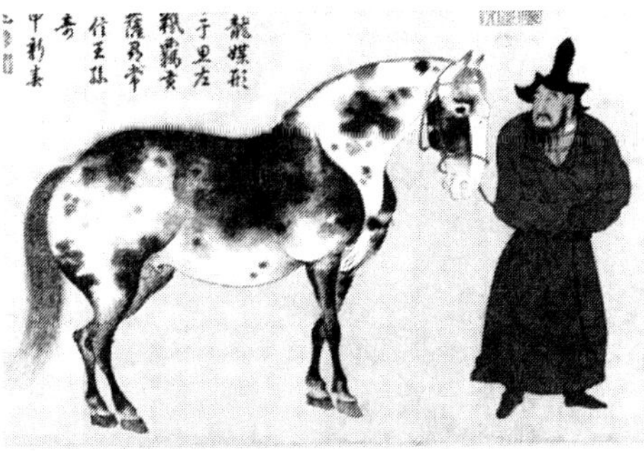

YUAN CAVALRYMAN

called Zhu Yuanzhang. In 1368, his army overthrew the Yuan dynasty and established the Ming dynasty. Though short-lived, the Yuan dynasty is remembered amongst the most important in Chinese history.

32 The Timurid Dynasty

An empire of Turkic-Mongol ethnicity, the Timurid dynasty was founded by Amir Timur Timurid (also known as Tamerlane), a descendant of Genghis Khan. The Timurid dynasty flourished from 1370 to 1857 CE.

1 After the death of Genghis Khan in 1227, his descendants started fighting for succession to the coveted Mongol throne. This resulted in the Mongol Empire fragmenting into multiple smaller parts. Chagatai Khan, the second son of Genghis Khan, took advantage of this and established the Chagatai Khanate, an empire spanning most of Central Asia. However, it was only when one of his descendants, Timur, ascended the throne that Chagatai's ultimate vision – to reunify the Mongol empire under the name of the Timurid dynasty – came to fruition. Timur took on the Muslim-Arabic title of 'Amir'. Following this, the Timurid Empire would rule and dominate Central Asia for more than a century.

2 In 1398, Timur launched an attack on Delhi. He conquered the Tughlaq dynasty of the Delhi Sultanate and appointed Khizr Khan, who was earlier a governor under the Tughlaqs, to rule on his behalf. Khizr's descendants eventually formed the Sayyid dynasty, the fourth one of the Delhi Sultanate. This dynasty became one of the most successful of the Sultanate, until it was defeated in 1451 by the Lodi dynasty. In 1402, Timur invaded the Ottoman Empire and had a major victory in the battle of Ankara. After Timur died in 1405, there were no important amirs until in 1526, Babur, a descendant of Timur, defeated Ibrahim Lodi of the Lodi sultanate in north India in the First Battle of Panipat and established the Mughal Empire.

ILLUSTRATION FROM *JAMI'S ROSE GARDEN OF THE PIOUS* BLENDS MINIATURE PAINTING AND POETRY IN A STYLE TYPICAL OF THE TIMURID EMPIRE

3 In 1507, the Timurid Empire collapsed due to invasions and the growing influence of the Safavid dynasty from Iran. In 1858, the Mughal

Empire declined, due to attacks by the Marathas, and later the British East India Company took over their territories during the reign of the last Mughal emperor, Bahadur Shah Zafar.

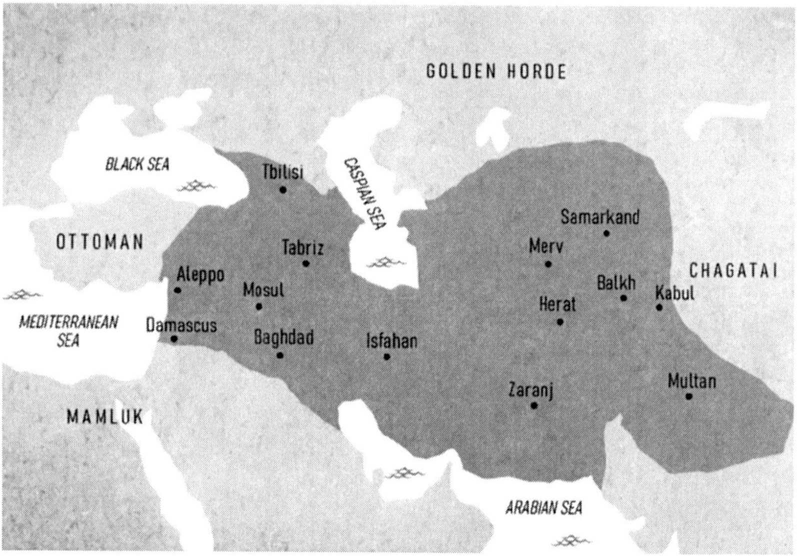

THE TIMURID EMPIRE

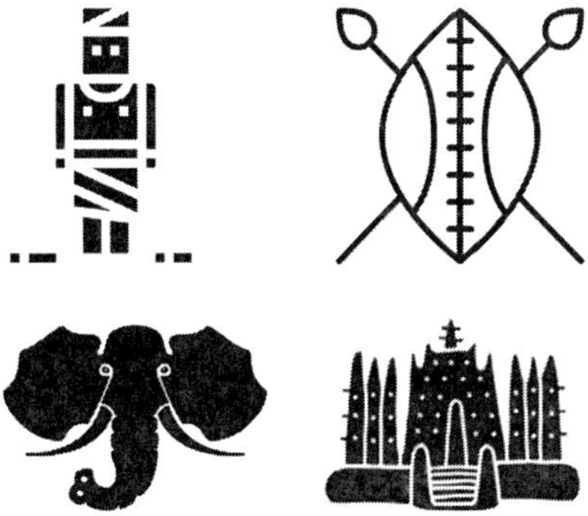

AFRICAN EMPIRES

33 The Kushite Empire

This legendary empire, also known as the kingdom of Kush, was located on the borders of modern-day Sudan and Egypt. It existed for more than a thousand years, from 1070 BCE until 300 CE.

1 During 1700 BCE, Kush was the most powerful kingdom in the Nile Valley, but was soon conquered by Egypt. However, by around the 11th century BCE, Kushite kings grew more powerful, united territories and established authority over the region. By the eighth century BCE, King Kashta, an influential ruler, and his son Piye, conquered many territories of the Egyptians, their arch-rivals.

2 The Kushites were renowned for their advancements in art. Despite their enmity, they were deeply influenced by the Egyptians. Like the Egyptians, they built pyramids, erected statues dedicated to their monarchs and even had their own hieroglyphics. An advanced civilization in its own right, Kush was a complex urban society centred on trading and (gold) mining even before urbanization came to Egypt. They also had a unique language.

Quite unlike the times, they encouraged the participation of women in all walks of life – even as monarchs. They developed technologies for storing and transporting water, pioneered an ancient form of antibiotics and had knowledge of trigonometry.

A KUSH PRINCE SLAYING HIS ENEMIES

3 In the first two centuries CE, Kush power waned due to their battles with Egypt, by then a Roman territory. Their traditional sources of wealth, iron and gold, also depleted. Around 300 CE they embarked on a campaign against the powerful Aksumites, hoping to monopolize their trade in ivory. However, this was the last straw – Kush defeat brought an end to the empire.

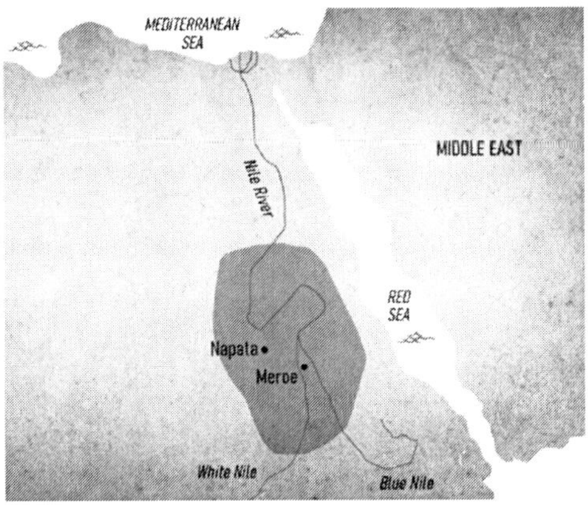

KUSH EMPIRE TERRITORIES

34 The Aksumite Empire

A civilization that existed in modern-day northern Ethiopia and Eritrea from 80 BCE to 825 CE, the Aksumite Empire was considered alongside Babylon, Rome and China as one of the four greatest powers of the time.

1 The Aksumite Civilization flourished along the banks of the Red Sea. They developed Africa's only indigenously formed written script called the Ge'ez. Aksumites were mostly herders, agriculturists and traders. They grew grains like wheat and barley, and raised cattle, sheep and camels. They initially

THE KING OF AKSUM WITH A MECCAN DELEGATION, MANUSCRIPT ILLUSTRATION

practised polytheism and Judaism, but adopted Christianity around 325 CE.

2 The Aksumite Empire was rich in gold and iron deposits and hence they gained their power through trading these commodities. They established commercial relationships with Rome, Egypt, Persia and India, where large quantities of ivory, gold, emeralds, iron and salt were traded. The Aksumites emerged as the greatest market in north-eastern Africa and dominated the Red Sea trade routes. To support their trading, the Aksumites developed their own currency system and minted their own coins. At the height of its power, around the fourth and fifth centuries CE, the Aksumite Empire extended across most of modern-day Eritrea, northern Ethiopia, western Yemen, southern Saudi Arabia, and Sudan. It also developed a strong alliance with the Byzantine Empire, as both these empires followed Christianity.

A PORTRAIT OF MARK THE EVANGELIST, ETHIOPIA

3 Around the sixth century CE, the Aksumite Empire started to collapse mainly because of overpopulation. Large-scale soil erosion began to occur, owing to the intensification of farming. With the rise of the Rashidun Caliphate and their taking control of the Red Sea, the Aksumite Empire's trade activities began to see a fast decline, leading to its ultimate collapse.

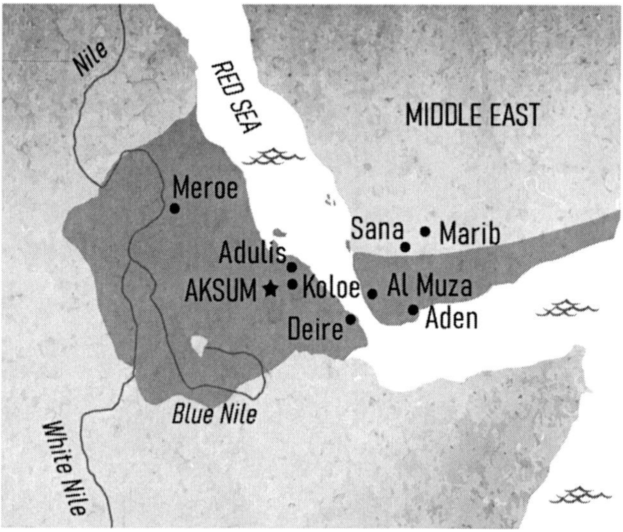

THE AKSUMITE EMPIRE

35 Carthage

Being the capital of the Carthaginian civilization, Carthage was a powerful and affluent city state that existed from 814 to 146 BCE located in present-day Tunisia.

1 Legend has it that the city of Carthage was founded by the Phoenicians from the city of Tyre, a dominant maritime power of the time, in search of wealthy lands that would help expand their businesses. They found Carthage, rich in resources like metals and agricultural produce and strategically located at the Gulf of Tunis, fit to be a trading post. After Alexander the Great's destruction of Tyre in 332 BCE, rich Phoenician refugees flocked to Carthage, made it their home and established it as a centre of trade.

2 The people of Carthage demonstrated great skills in agriculture, veterinary science and animal husbandry. They also developed a unique style of architecture, where houses rose six storeys high around a central courtyard with its own cistern and drainage system. They developed technology

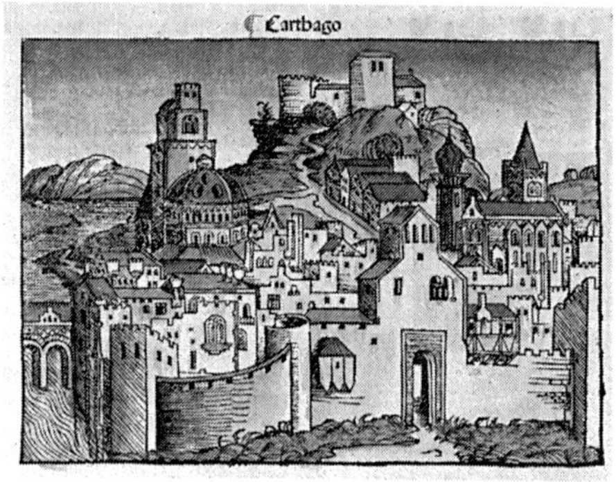

ARTIST'S IMPRESSION OF CARTHAGE FROM THE 1493 *NUREMBERG CHRONICLE*

similar to the Roman aqueducts to transport water. Their towns were also precisely organized, with beautiful buildings, houses and temples.

3 From 264 BCE, Carthage was involved in several conflicts with Rome, another rising power, which came to be known as the Punic Wars. In the First Punic War (264–241 BCE), Rome proved to be a great adversary, defeating Carthage and taking control of some of its territories. During the Second Punic War (218 to 202 BCE), the great Carthaginian general, Hannibal, gained eminence. Though he won his greatest victory in 216 BCE, he was eventually defeated by the Romans. In the Third

Punic War (149–146 BCE), the Romans besieged the city and then burned it to the ground.

ROME AND CARTHAGE AT THE START OF THE SECOND PUNIC WAR

36 The Almoravid Dynasty

Founded initially as an Islamic religious movement based in modern-day Morocco, the Almoravid dynasty existed from 1040 to 1147 CE.

1 The Almoravids were Berbers, descendants of pre-Arab peoples of North Africa. The dynasty was founded by Yahya ibn Ibrahim, in 1040 CE, along with a missionary, Abdulla Ibn Yasin, to preach a pure form of Islam. Gathering followers, by 1054 CE they captured the western Saharan trade routes. Their first conquest was the Morocco region. They were invited by other Muslim rulers of the region to raise a defence against the Christian armies of northern Spain. After defeating the Christians, they overthrew the Muslim rulers too, controlling most of modern Spain and Portugal, and assuming the title of Emir al Muslimin (Commander of Muslims). At the empire's peak, they ruled Morocco, Mauritania, Algeria, Senegal, Mali, Spain and Portugal.

2 The Almoravids set up major urban centres in Morocco, including the cities of Marrakech and Fes. They built great mosques, urban

gardens and defensive walls. Their architectural innovations used cusped arches and decorative motifs. They are known for their beautiful Koubbas - burial sites with Islamic-style shrines on top - the most famous being the Koubba in Morocco.

3 In the early 1100s they faced a revolt from rival Berbers, the Almohads, while at their borders they were at war with Christian armies. The empire fell in 1147 CE.

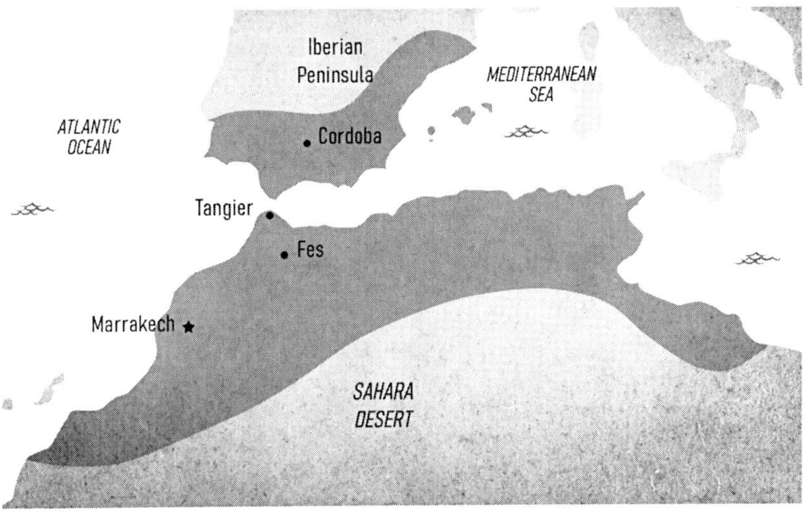

THE ALMORAVID TERRITORIES

37 The Almohad Caliphate

Similar to the Almoravid dynasty that they replaced, the Almohads were also a Berber Islamic dynasty. They reigned between 1147 and 1269 CE.

1 The founder of the Almohad dynasty was Ibn Tumart, a staunch Islamist with his own ideology of Islam. He gained followers among his tribe in Morocco and established a Caliphate. They opposed the religious teachings propagated by the Almoravids and revolted against them, eventually replacing them. During the early part of their rule, the Almohads took over present-day Morocco, Algeria, Tunisia, and several parts of Libya and the Iberian Peninsula. They retained Marrakech, the capital of the Almoravids, as their power centre but made Seville in Al-Andalus their capital.

2 The Almohad Caliphate's contributions to art and architecture were centred around their religious beliefs. In Marrakech, they constructed the grand mosques of Koutoubia, Tinmel and Qasba. and the famed Menara gardens. In Seville, they built the Great Mosque and a minaret called La Giralda.

In the arts and textiles, they popularized heavily ornamental styles, geometric designs and a style of cursive Maghrebi script. Evidence of this is found in their manuscripts, coinage and architecture.

3 The Almohad dynasty began to decline in early 1200 CE, after being defeated by the combined Christian armies of Aragon and Castil, two influential Spanish kingdoms. This was aggravated by internal problems, such as dictatorial rulers and intolerance towards Christians and Jews.

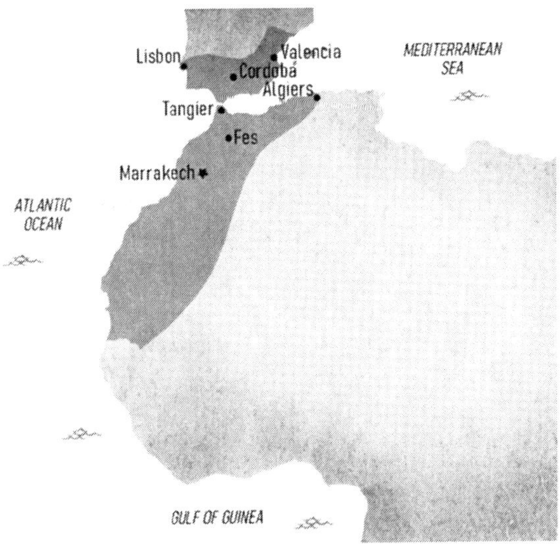

THE ALMOHAD EMPIRE

38 The Mali Empire

One of the wealthiest empires in Africa and possibly the whole world at the time, the Mali Empire existed from 1235 to 1600 CE.

1 The Mali Empire originated when Sundiata Keita, also known as the 'Lion King', united the various tribes of Mali and successfully revolted and killed a cruel emperor, Soumaoro Kanté, of the Sasso Empire, a kingdom of West Africa, who was at war with Mali. Sundiata ascended the throne and assumed the title of Mansa, or ruler of Mali.

2 The Mali Empire was known for its large possession of gold dust and had three large gold mines. It became so wealthy and famous that the traders were taxed even to enter their kingdom. The greatest king of Mali was Mansa Musa I who reigned for 25 years from 1312 CE. Under him, the empire expanded in territories, trade, wealth and culture. Learning centres, schools, universities and libraries were established across the empire, making it multilingual and multi-ethnic. He established Sankore University, an ancient centre of learning in

MALIAN ARCHITECTURE

Timbuktu, Mali, with the largest collection of books in Africa. Many historians believe that Mansa Musa could have been the richest man in the history of the

THE CATALAN ATLAS FEATURES MANSA MUSA

world, so much so that during his Mecca pilgrimage in 1324, he gave out such large quantities of gold that it depreciated in value for the next decade.

3 After Mansa Musa's death in 1337, the empire started to decline, coinciding with the emergence of other kingdoms including the Songhai Empire. Mali was constantly under attack from the Mossi people of Burkina Faso and the Tuareg people. By the late 15th century, most of the territories of the great Mali Empire were captured by the Songhai Empire.

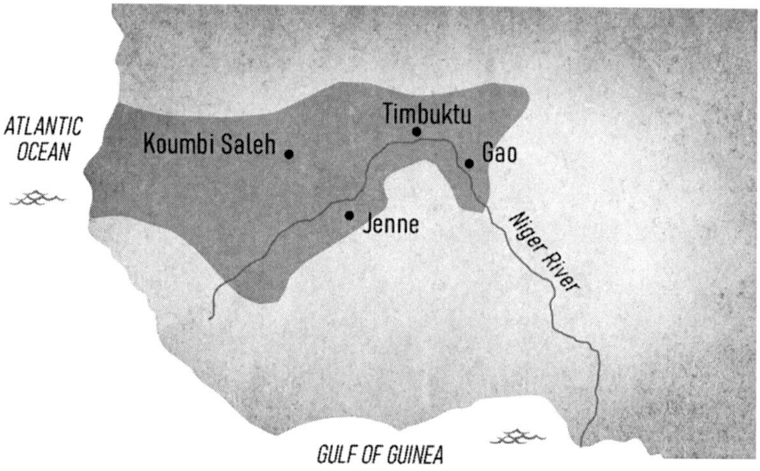

■ THE MALI EMPIRE

39 The Songhai Empire

This African empire, established in modern-day Mali, lasted from 1464 to 1591 CE.

1 The Songhai people were mainly based in the city of Gao along the River Niger from 800 CE. Mali added this prosperous city to their empire in 1325. The turning point came with the Songhai prince, Sunni Ali, being taken prisoner by the Mali Empire. He escaped in 1464, captured Gao, and later conquered the key trading cities of Timbuktu and Djenne, thus establishing the Songhai Empire.

2 The Songhai Empire reached its zenith in the reign of Muhammad I Askia (Askia the Great). Large tracts of the Mali Empire were captured, making the Songhai one of the largest empires in African history. They had access to major ports, trading in palm oil, ivory, slaves, spices and precious

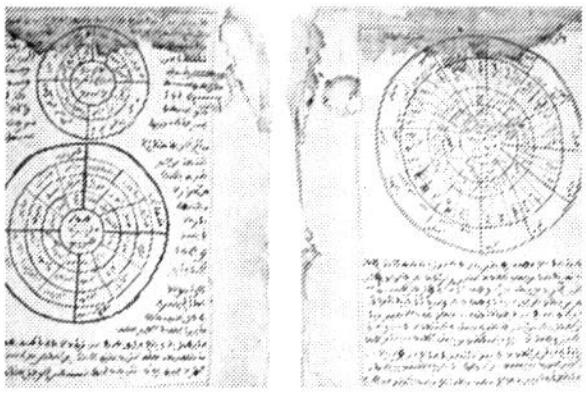

THE TIMBUKTU MANUSCRIPTS, MORE THAN 70,000 OF THEM, SHOW VAST KNOWLEDGE OF ART, MEDICINE, PHILOSOPHY AND SCIENCE

woods in exchange for cloth, salt, horses, arms and armour. Culture and art flourished, making Songhai a hub of artists, artisans and inventors. They developed a special fusion of Islamic and African styles in architecture and ceramics.

3 The empire began to decline around the late 1500s due to internal strife. The Moroccan army, led by Judar Pasha, invaded it in 1591 and the empire fell with the battle of Tondibi.

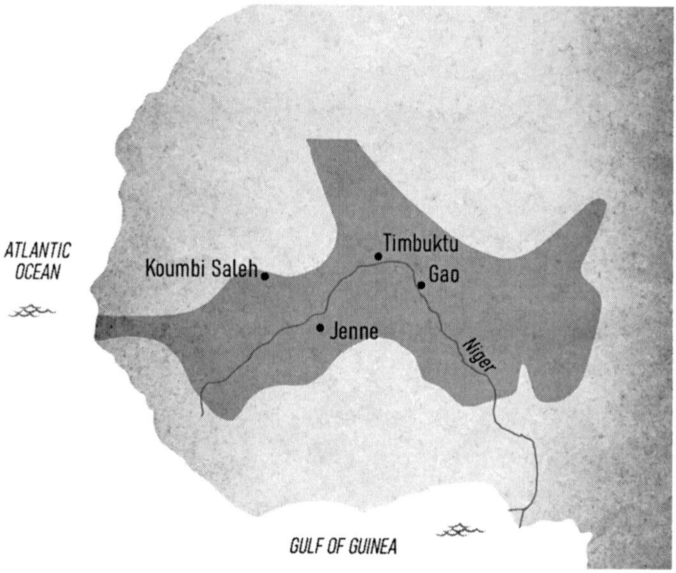

■ SONGHAI TERRITORIES

40 The Funj Sultanate

The Funj Sultanate, also called the Black Sultanate, lasted from 1504 to 1821 CE in present-day Democratic Republic of Sudan.

1 The Funj dynasty is presumed to have come from the upper Blue Nile region. In 1504, Amara Dunqas, a Funj leader, founded the Black Sultanate with Sennar as the capital. Its population mainly comprised the Nubian, Arab and Beja peoples, who mostly spoke Arabic and practised Islam.

2 The sultanate flourished in the 17th and 18th centuries, reaching its height under King Badi II Abu Daqn. It spanned the Nile Valley from the Egypt border to the mouth of the Blue Nile, even inhibiting Ottoman expansion. They had contacts with south

A FUNJ KING OF SENNAR

and central Sudan, and an economy thriving on slave trade. Philosophers from Egypt introduced Islamic theology and religious courts here.

THE MOSQUE OF SENNAR

3 By end-1700 CE, the dynasty waned, with a Funj army chieftain carrying out a coup. The sultan was reduced to a figurehead and vassal states flouted his authority. In 1821, the Funj surrendered in a battle to the Ottoman viceroy of Egypt, Mehmet Ali.

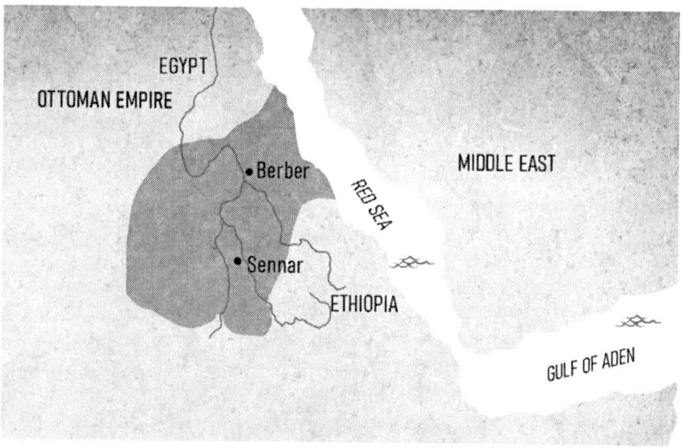

THE FUNJ EMPIRE

SOUTH AMERICAN EMPIRES

41 The Caral-Supe Civilization

Also known as the Norte Chico Civilization, the Caral-Supe existed in north-central coastal Peru from 3500 to 1700 BCE. It is the oldest known civilization in the Americas.

1 Caral, considered the oldest urban centre in the Americas, spread across around 150 acres of coastal lands. Its nearly 3,000 inhabitants were mostly skilled fishermen and farmers. Initially a conglomeration of tribes, it developed larger hierarchical systems. It is suggested that 19 other sites around the main site could have been part of the same civilization, with almost 20,000 people in all.

2 Due to their prehistoric origin, written evidence about the Caral-Supe is scanty. Use of cotton played an important role in their development as it helped them to make fishing nets and textiles. The civilization is known for its

CARAL-SUPE PYRAMID

pyramids, mostly used for religious and ceremonial purposes, found in old Caral sites. The main pyramid is called the Templo Mayor, a 490 feet long and 180 feet high truncated pyramid. Notably, these pyramids were built over 100 years before the Egyptian ones and more than 4,000 years before the Aztec ones. The civilization is also known for its great sculptures, carved onto the walls of buildings, or on clay. A 3,800-year-old wall from the Caral Civilization has the carving of an octopus-like creature.

THE CARAL-SUPE EMPIRE

3 Around 1800 BCE, the civilization began to decline, possibly due to the rise of more powerful civilizations in the Andes region.

42 The Olmec Civilization

The first major civilization in Mexico, the Olmecs were prominent from 1400 to 500 BCE.

1 Though it is unclear where the Olmecs came from, some theories propose China or Africa. The Olmecs lived in the tropical lowlands near the Gulf of Mexico. The Olmec Civilization is an archaeological culture, as we know of their existence

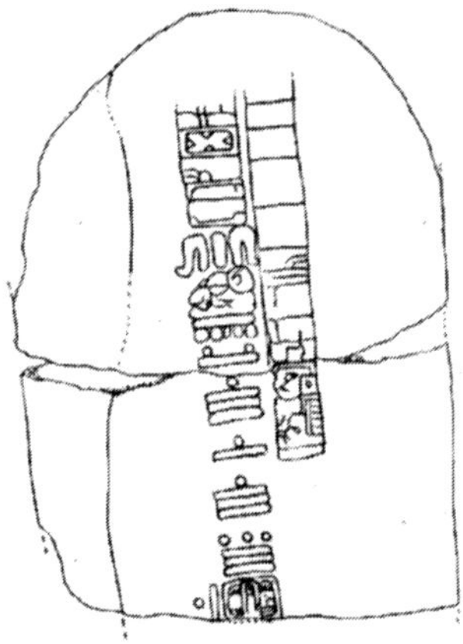

A STEELE IN AN OLMEC SCRIPT HAS THE SECOND OLDEST LONG COUNT DATE, WITH THE NUMERALS 7.16.6.16.18 TRANSLATING TO 3 SEPTEMBER 32 BCE

from the artefacts, buildings and monuments they left behind. They used jade, volcanic rocks, pottery, mica and rubber, which have been found across Meso-America (the central region of America, from central Mexico to Nicaragua). This is perhaps indicative of the extensive trading activities of this civilization. Each Olmec site found featured an elaborate complex of temples, pyramids, altars, stone sculptures and tombs.

2 The most famous among all the artefacts left behind by the Olmecs are colossal heads, carved from stone, and weighing around two tonnes on average. Till date, 17 heads have been unearthed. Olmecs are also believed to be the first set of people to figure out how to convert latex into rubber that could be shaped and hardened to produce balls used in ceremonial games. They made and traded rubber throughout Meso-America. Urban planning assigned small houses for commoners and larger houses for the elites. Their cities also included large pyramids to honour their gods.

A COLOSSAL OLMEC HEAD

3 The Olmec Civilization is thought to have been the mother civilization for many others that followed, including the Mayan and the Zapotec. Around 500 BCE, the Olmec Civilization started to decline. Historians believe that it could have been due to environmental changes leading to depopulation, or because of increased volcanic activity in the region, leading to the relocation of settlements.

■ THE OLMEC EMPIRE

43 The Chavin Civilization

Located in the Andean highland of Peru, the Chavin Civilization flourished between 900 to 200 BCE, roughly 1,000 years after the Caral Civilization.

1 The civilization grew around their temple known as Chavin de Huantar. For the first 400 years or so, only a few hundred people lived around the temple, which was the regional and ceremonial centre of the civilization. After 500 BCE, the civilization experienced a point of inflection, when the population increased, urban societies came up, the temple was remodelled, trade relationships multiplied and economy progressed.

A CHAVIN VESSEL

2 During the period around 500 BCE, llamas were domesticated and the rich economy began to depend on llama-jerky (dried meat) trade. The Chavins successfully grew crops like potato, maize and quinoa. They developed an irrigation system to control floods and kept their crops

hydrated throughout the year. The Chavins are also known for their great art and architecture. The Chavin heads, sculptured from stone and inserted into the walls of temples, called tenon heads, were made approximately around 4,000 years ago – one such site is near the town of Chupacoto. The Chavins are also known for their great steles and obelisks, including the Raimondi stele and the Lanzon in the Old Temple of Chavin de Huantar. The Tello obelisk is known as the most complex piece of art of the time.

THE CHAVIN EMPIRE

3 Around 200 BCE, the Chavin Civilization began depopulating and declining. It is believed that several years of successive droughts and earthquakes in Chavin could have caused a social upheaval, resulting in the fall of the civilization.

44

The Zapotec Civilization

The Zapotec Civilization, located in central Meso-America in the valley of Oaxaca in present-day South America, flourished from 700 BCE to 1527 CE.

1 The Zapotecs originated from small agricultural communities that established themselves in the valleys around Oaxaca in 700 BCE. Around 100 BCE onwards, Zapotec rulers started to conquer and colonize provinces outside the valley. By 200 CE, the Zapotecs built Monte Alban, their initial settlement that eventually grew to be their largest city, and retained this status until around 700 CE.

2 The Zapotecs are known best for their hieroglyphics, a logo-syllabic script and their precise calendar. In art and architecture, they flattened mountaintops, created open spaces and built beautiful pyramidical temples with steps on the sides, their railings supported by large

ZAPOTEC RUINS IN MITLA, MEXICO

balusters. A great example is the Monte Alban site in Mexico, with plazas, passageways, pyramids and tombs. Zapotec sculptures were made of clay and jade, depicting jaguars, gods, bears and snakes. They followed a polytheistic religion, with gods mainly associated with farming and fertility.

3 From 1497 to 1502, the Zapotecs were engaged in battles with their rival civilization, the Aztecs. When the Spanish invaders landed, they were in a weakened state. The Spanish took advantage of this and defeated them in a five-year-long war that ended in 1527.

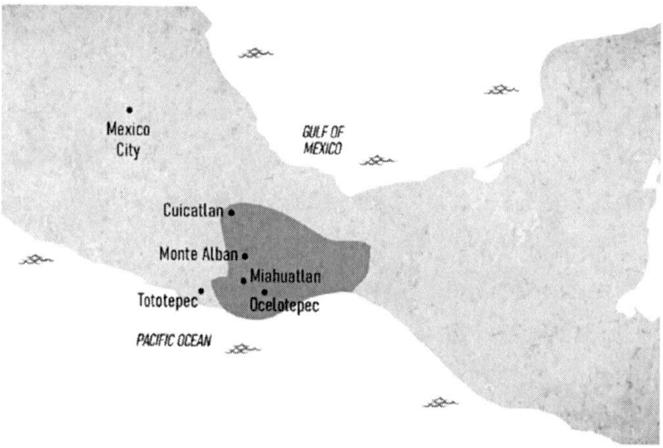

■ THE ZAPOTEC EMPIRE

45 The Nazca Civilization

Located on Peru's southern coast, this civilization was centred around Nazca and its surrounding valleys. It lasted between 100 and 800 CE after the Wari Civilization in the same region.

1 The Nazca settlement was planned in a unique manner, divided into ceremonial sites, and habitation areas. It developed as local chiefdoms around the Cahuachi ceremonial site, which had many beautiful pyramidical temples made of mounds of stones. The habitation sites had small villages, with houses using a framework of poles and mud plaster. They built large burial sites with resin, stone and mud bricks, where mummies have been found, as in the Chauchilla cemetery used for over 600 years.

2 The Nazcas are known most for their 'Nazca lines' – geometric patterns carved into the ground possibly by making depressions in the desert floor, thus exposing differently coloured particles. These geoglyphs, around 400 to 1,000 metres across, have patterns of animals and plants.

They may have had a ceremonial or calendar-keeping purpose. Nazca multicoloured pottery, painted with mythical animals and geometric patterns, is also well known.

A SITE OF THE MYSTERIOUS NAZCA LINES

3 Around 750 CE, the civilization began to depopulate and decline, probably due to frequent floods. In 800 CE, the civilization ended.

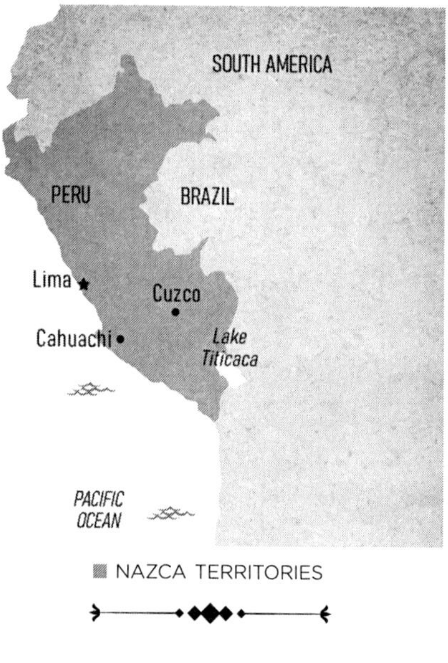

NAZCA TERRITORIES

46 The Wari Civilization

Flourishing in the coastal and highland areas of Peru, the Wari Civilization existed between 450 and 1000 CE.

1 The Wari civilization, at its peak, had a population of almost 70,000 people spread across 15 square kilometres. They made great advancements in agriculture, including the construction of canals to

THE WARI EMPIRE

irrigate terraced fields. Their superior skills in land management helped them tide over decades of drought in the region. Wari architecture included D-shaped temples, rectangular houses, doubled-storey buildings and massive, 10-metre-high walls. Mud mortar was used for building and was painted white. They built a large network of roads, which were also used by the Incas afterwards.

2 The Waris were also known for their art and textiles. They wove stunning tunics and hats with colourful geometric patterns. They used camelid fibre, mainly hair from local animals such as llamas and alpacas. The Waris made sculptures and figurines from gold and ivory, and painted clay pots.

3 Around 800 CE, the Wari civilization was affected by a series of severe droughts, made worse by constant political infighting. Once the political system collapsed, the civilization could not stand. After almost 200 years of continued droughts and war, the civilization ended.

WARI EARFLARES, LARGE TRUMPET-SHAPED EAR ORNAMENTS

47 The Aztec Empire

Having established a strong and prosperous empire located in modern-day Mexico, the Aztecs flourished from 1345 to 1521 CE.

1 A nomadic people who traced their origins to northern Mexico, the Aztecs eventually settled on a small island in Lake Texcoco, which later emerged as Tenochtitlan, now the historic centre of Mexico City. This was initially one of the many small

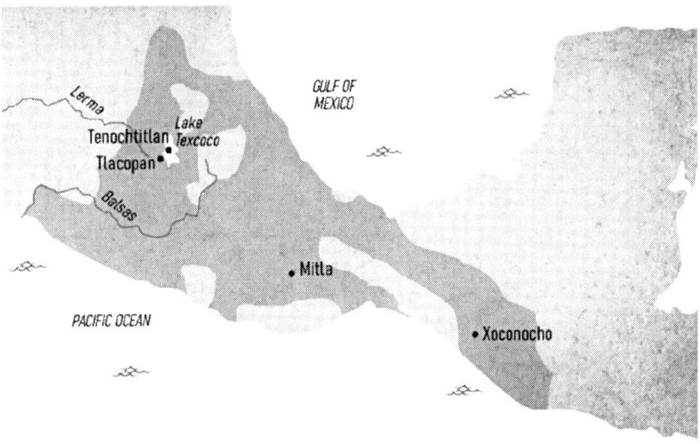

AZTEC EXPANSION OVER THE YEARS

city states in the region, but under the ruler Itzcoatl, in 1428 CE, the Aztecs formed a strong three-way alliance with the neighbouring Texcocans and the Tacubans, resulting in an empire that dominated central Mexico. They invaded their powerful rivals including the Tepanecs and Tlaxcala, and by the early 16th century, ruled over hundreds of small states with over six million inhabitants.

2 The Aztecs developed superior techniques in agriculture, helping them sustain a large population. They had a planned system for irrigation, similar to aqueducts, which could pump water and irrigate the entire region. The Aztecs also made discoveries in medicine, using local flora and fauna for their medicinal properties to make ointments and medical concoctions. Chocolate in its basic form, as a bitter drink brewed from cacao beans, was first consumed by the Aztecs. They even used the beans as their currency. They excelled in architecture,

A *TLACOCHCALCATL* OR AZTEC GENERAL AS SHOWN IN THE CODEX MENDOZA

evidenced in their pyramids, some of the largest in the region, dedicated to the sun and the moon. Aztec artefacts, such as the calendar stone, are today housed in museums across the globe. The Aztecs had also devised a solar calendar, similar to the modern-day one, comprising 365 days.

3 However, in 1519, the Spanish conquistador Hernán Cortés arrived in Mexico, looking for gold. He captured the Aztec king Montezuma II and imprisoned him. This shook the foundations of the empire. In 1521 CE, the Spanish conquistadors unleashed terror in the region until the locals surrendered. Hereafter, the Spanish recklessly looted and gutted the region

HERNÁN CORTÉS AND MALINCHE (FAR RIGHT) LEADING THE SPANISH ARMY THAT CONQUERED MEXICO

48 The Inca Empire

A prosperous and wealthy empire, the largest in pre-Columbian America, the Inca Empire was located along the Pacific coast and Andean highlands. It existed from 1438 to 1533 CE.

1 Formerly a pastoral people, the Incas lived in the Cusco (or Cuzco) region of Peru, and were united by Manco Capac, the founder of the Inca Empire. The kingdom started out as a small city state called Cusco. It expanded the most under its ninth emperor, Pachacuti, who extended the empire throughout the Andes Mountains and reorganized it into what is called Tahuantinsuyu, or the land of four quarters. It had a central government with the Inca emperor as its head and four provinces under governors. During its peak, the Inca Empire stretched to include parts of present-

MANCO CAPAC, THE FOUNDER AND FIRST GOVERNOR OF THE INCA EMPIRE

day Ecuador, Chile, Peru, Bolivia, Argentina and Columbia, housing more than 12 million inhabitants.

2 The Incas were master builders and constructors. They built a network of highways covering over 40,000 kilometres, enabling them to control their vast empire. They also devised a centralized religion and language to unify their empire, which had more than 100 ethnic groups. They used a system of mortarless construction with a technique called dry-stone, in which the stones fitted together as if they were one. They constructed impressive temples, including the Temple of the Sun in Cusco. The famed Machu Picchu, one of the seven wonders of the world, is an Incan citadel, in which temples and fortifications were carved out of vast boulders. The Incas were also known for their rich art and textiles. They made loincloths and winter cloaks with cotton and wool. Their rich sources of gold allowed them to develop their skill to sculpt metals. The Incas also had a rich and flourishing trading

MACHU PICCHU, THE FAMOUS INCAN CITADEL

culture, where they exchanged goods, such as exotic foods, cloth, metal, meat, wool and even feathers. Trade made the Incas one of the richest economies of the time.

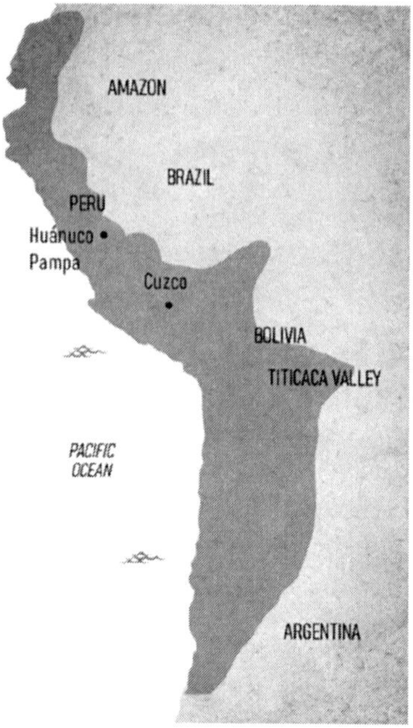

THE INCA EMPIRE

3 With the arrival of the Spanish explorers with their muskets and cannons, the Incas began to see a decline. In 1533 CE, the Spanish launched a surprise attack on the Incas, taking over most of their regions. The Spanish also carried diseases like the smallpox that wiped out large populations of the Incas.

FAMILIES AND DYNASTIES

49 The Julio-Claudian Dynasty

Comprising the first five emperors of Rome – Augustus, Tiberius, Caligula, Claudius and Nero – the Julio-Claudian dynasty ruled from 27 BCE to 68 CE.

1 After the death of Julius Caesar, his adopted son, Octavius Caesar, won a civil war, adopted the name Augustus and ruled Rome as the first emperor of the Julio-Claudian dynasty. Though a family, none of the emperors gave the throne to their sons. For example, Tiberius was Augustus's stepson, and Caligula was Tiberius's grand-nephew.

2 The dynasty conquered most of modern-day Europe, including Pannonia, Germania, Dalmatia and Raetia. During Augustus's reign many theatres and temples, including those of Mars and Apollo, were built. Public entertainment included many festivals and games. Though initially architecture took on a Hellenistic style, with monumental columns, using terracotta, during Claudius's reign, a more Roman style emerged with domes and arches. Literature featured stalwarts like

Horace, Ovid and Virgil. The dynasty ushered in the 'Pax Romana', a period of stability and prosperity across the empire.

3 Augustus Caesar's administrative, economic and military reforms stabilized the Roman Empire. His successors were weak, including the last ruler, Nero, who died by suicide. 'The year of four emperors' followed, with civil wars and quick changes of rulers. The fourth one, Vespasian, took the throne and established the Flavian dynasty.

AUGUSTUS, TIBERIUS, CALIGULA, CLAUDIUS AND NERO – EMPERORS OF THE JULIO-CLAUDIAN DYNASTY.

50 The Capetian Dynasty

A powerful family in Europe, the Capetian Dynasty ruled France for over 800 years, from 987 to 1792 CE, until monarchy was abolished in France.

1 Before the Capetians came to power, another family called the Carolingians, to which emperor Charlamagne belonged, ruled France. The Carolingians were weakened considerably during late 800 CE due to incompetence and Viking attacks. Hence in 987 CE, Hugh Capet, the son of a powerful

KING HUGH CAPET, FOUNDER OF THE CAPETIAN DYNASTY

duke, was elected to succeed Louis V of the Carolingian dynasty, who died childless. The empire that Hugh Capet inherited was rather small, but over time, they increased their wealth through the major dioceses and abbeys they controlled, allowing them to extend their power and territories across Europe, including present-day Italy, France and Spain. Though France had an elective monarchy, during the time of the early Capetian kings, they made it a mere formality paving the way for a system of hereditary succession, where the elder son would inherit the throne.

2 The Capetians enabled the development of many administrative institutions of the French monarchy, including the representative assembly and the courts. Among the many Capetian rulers, outstanding ones were: Philip II Augustus, who ruled from 1180 to 1223 CE, capturing territories held by England; and Louis IX, who ruled from 1226 to 1270 CE, responsible for negotiating a peace treaty with the English, modernizing the administrative system and reducing corruption among royal officials. Louis IX ushered in a golden age for France, during which literature, art and architecture made great strides. Great buildings, such as the Sainte-Chapelle,

Louis's personal royal chapel, a great example of Rayonnant Gothic architecture using smaller structures compared to the High Gothic cathedrals, were commissioned. During Philip IV's reign (1285–1314 CE), Paris became the capital of France, as he centralized his government and departments there, and its university grew in prominence. The French language developed by producing many great literature pieces, including the chansons. Under the Capetians, France emerged as one of the greatest powers in Europe.

3 The direct line of the Capetian dynasty came to an end in 1328 CE. Until then a long sequence of rulers in this dynasty produced 15 kings, laying the foundations for the French nation state. However, branches of the Capetians – the Valois and the Bourbons – ruled until 1793, after which the French Revolution abolished the hereditary monarchy of the dynasty. Many descendants of the Capetian dynasty ruled regions beyond France, including three emperors who ruled Constantinople.

51 The House of Plantagenet

Also known as the House of Anjou, the House of Plantagenet was a royal family that ruled England for over 300 years from 1154 to 1485 CE.

1 The Royal House originated as a small kingdom located in a small province, called Anjou, in France. During Henry II rule (1154–1189 CE), the borders of his kingdom stretched from south-west France to Scotland. By the end of its rule, in 1485 CE, the House of Plantagenet had taken over almost all of Europe under its rule including France, Britain, Ireland and the Duchy of Normandy.

HENRY II, THE FIRST PLANTAGENET KING OF ENGLAND

2 Under the Plantagenets, there was an overall transformation of England. John, King of England from 1199 to 1216 CE, signed the Magna Carta, laying the foundations

for English law. One of the greatest kings in the House of Plantagenet was Edward I (reign: 1272-1307 CE), who brought in many reforms and overall stability. Edward developed the institution of the parliament, which became a model, consisting of representatives from the barons, knights, clergy and the townspeople. To promote uniform and just administration, Edward I cut down the feudal privileges and established the rights of the Crown, thereby reinstating a sophisticated system of justice, which started with the Magna Carta. Under the Plantagenet, a distinct national identity started emerging, and English was established as the primary language.

3 In the later years, the House of Plantagenet's two branches - York and Lancaster - engaged in battles of bitter rivalry that led to the Wars of the Roses. This culminated in the Battle of Bosworth Field in 1485 CE, when the last king of the Plantagenets, King Richard III, was killed. This brought an end to the dynasty. Hereafter, Henry VII, from the Lancastrian branch, took over the throne and started a new dynasty, the Tudors.

52 The Shimazu Family

A warrior clan of Japan, the Shimazu family initially controlled only a part of Kyushu Island, but later became influential across the whole of Japan. It existed from 1179 to 1587 CE.

1 The Shimazu family was established when a warlord named Shimazu Tadahisa became the governor of southern Kyushu Island in Japan. Later, the 16th head of the family unified the entire Kyushu area and the Shimazus allied with other powerful families, such as the Mori family in Choshu. In the 17th century, they invaded the Ryukyu kingdom, a tributary of imperial China, took over their maritime trade networks of east and South-East Asia and gained access to Chinese luxury goods. Their dominance in trade and warcraft helped the family emerge as a feared clan in all of Japan.

2 The Shimazu family used the Japanese feudal system to their advantage. Military service and support from the vassals enabled the Shimazu to win wars and gain power. In 1600, in the Battle of Sekigahara, the formidable Tokugawa

clan defeated the Western army, of which Shimazus were a part, to establish a shogunate from 1603. However, Shimazu warriors, along with allies, overthrew the shogunate in the political revolution of 1868 and the imperial Meiji Restoration. Emperor Meiji bestowed the hereditary rank of a prince on the family, allowing them to dominate the political sphere until the end of the First World War.

3 The Shimazu family was one of the most powerful clans in Japan, with a strong hold on political and economic power. They were uniquely the only family to have played a major role in both medieval and modern Japanese history.

SAMURAI OF THE SATSUMA CLAN, THE BOSHIN WAR PERIOD (1868-69)

53 The Clan of the Great Khan

A family of kings called the Khanates or the Clan of the Great Khan dominated most of the world from 1206 to 1368 CE.

1 The clan of the Great Khan was established when a man named Temujin rose from slavery to unite all the nomadic tribes in Mongolia under the Mongol Empire. He took the name Genghis Khan and the title 'The Great Khan'. A strong military leader, he led a series of conquests to eventually create one of the largest empires ever, spanning over 12 million square miles. He died in 1227 CE during a campaign against the Chinese kingdom of Xi Xia. The Mongol kingdom was then taken over by Genghis's third son, Ogedei Khan, who added Persia, Georgia, Armenia, Korea, the remaining parts of China and many parts of Europe to the empire. His son, Guyuk Khan, followed by Genghis's grandson, Mongke Khan, became the next Khans. With Mongke Khan's death in 1259 CE, a battle for succession, the Toluid civil war, broke out between his two younger brothers, Kublai Khan and Ariq Boke. Kublai won, but the Mongol Empire was permanently divided.

EIGHT OF THE 15 GREAT KHANS OF THE MONGOL EMPIRE

2 The Mongol Empire fragmented into four different pieces after the civil war for succession. In China, Kublai Khan, one of Genghis's grandsons, took over and founded the Yuan dynasty. Persia was ruled by the Ilkhanate, while in Asia, the Chagatai Khanate wielded power, bringing forth military leaders like Timur (whose descendant, Babur, later founded the Mughal Empire in India). In Eastern Europe, the Kipchak or Golden Horde ruled. These four separate parts of the earlier Mongol Empire came to be known as the

four Khanates. Despite the political fragmentation, the regions under the Khanates enjoyed a stable economy and social life, and a time of peace compared to almost a century previously ridden with conquests and civil wars. This period came to be referred to as Pax Mongolica. The Silk Road was unified, easing trade and commerce across the region. Strong Mongol militaries abolished local tax regimes and extortions, and eased the supply chains. The Mongols also entered into alliances with other kingdoms to ensure smooth trading systems. They also set up a postal relay system called the 'Yam' to communicate between various parts of their empires.

3 There might have been several reasons for the disintegration of the Khanates during the mid-14th century Mainly, wars between the Khanates, weak rulers, civil wars and even religious intolerance caused them to weaken. The Black Death or bubonic plague also played an important role, as many of the Khanate rulers succumbed to this. The pandemic spread rapidly through the busy and smooth trade routes, ultimately resulting in the disintegration of the Clan of the Great Khan and the end of Pax Mongolica.

54 The House of Habsburg

An Austrian royal dynasty, the House of Habsburg members were the hereditary rulers of the Holy Roman Empire, centred in modern-day Vienna. It existed from 1246 to 1918 CE.

1 The family was originally an obscure small duchy originating in Germany. However, in a battle with King Ottokar II of Bohemia, Rudolf I, one of the earliest Habsburgs, took possession of Austria and established the Habsburg Empire. The imperial title transformed into a hereditary one, enabling the Habsburgs to expand their kingdom not only through conquests but also through marriage alliances, inheritances and agreements. Eventually, during the next 650 years or so, they brought most of central and eastern Europe under their control.

2 Among the Habsburgs, the most successful ruler was Maximilian I, who ruled from 1486 to 1519 CE. He expanded the influence of the family through his marriage to Mary of Burgundy, the ruler of the Burgundian State, and his son's

marriage to the Queen of Castile and Aragon. Like his father, he ruled over the Holy Roman Empire. He patronized art and literature, supporting and employing several artists. His grandson, Charles V (reign: 1519–56), was another great ruler from the dynasty, who managed to thwart the expansion of the Ottoman Turks in central Europe and captured Tunis in North Africa. He sponsored Ferdinand Magellan, the Portuguese navigator, to circumnavigate the earth, Hernan Cortes to conquer the Aztecs in Mexico and Francisco Pizarro to subdue the Incas in Peru. He continued the patronage of arts and literature. In fact, the fine arts were so important to the Habsburgs that one of their rulers, Rudolf II (reign: 1576–1612 CE), was an able painter, the Archduke of Austria, Charles II (reign 1564–90 CE), was a talented woodworker.

MAXIMILIAN I, A PORTRAIT

3 The Habsburgs started to collapse due to the ineptitude of some of their later rulers, resulting in widespread famines, food

shortages and deaths in their territories. Influenced by the Bolsheviks' victory in Russia, the Austrians started to revolt against the dynasty. There were rebellions in the army and the navy. The First World War worsened this decline, and on 11 November 1918, the last Habsburg ruler, Charles I, relinquished the throne and dissolved the Habsburg monarchy.

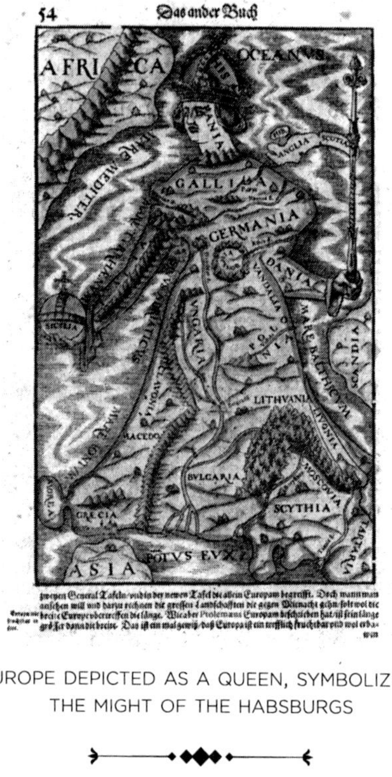

EUROPE DEPICTED AS A QUEEN, SYMBOLIZING THE MIGHT OF THE HABSBURGS

55 The House of Osman

Also known as the Osmanoglu family, the House of Osman was the longest ruling dynasty in the history of Islam, reigning from 1299 to 1922 CE.

1 The House of Osman comprised the emperors of the Ottoman dynasty. Originating from the Kayi tribe branch of the Oghuz Turks, the family started with Osman I from Anatolia, who laid the foundation of the Ottoman Empire, ruling from 1299 to 1324 CE. He consolidated many tribal regions, then laid siege to the fortress of Kulaca Hisar in present-day Turkey, against Byzantium, in the first castle conquest for the Ottomans. They later conquered Yenisehir in Turkey, which became the capital. In 1326, Osman died, leaving a flourishing empire, which expanded across Europe under his successors, all members of the House of Osman.

2 In over 620 years, as many as 36 sultans from the House of Ottoman ruled over the empire. However, the first ruler to officially take the title of sultan was Murad I (reign: 1359–89 CE), and the Ottoman state officially became an empire

once Sultan Mehmet II, or Mehmet the Conqueror (reign 1444–46 CE and 1451–81 CE), laid siege to Constantinople and made it the capital. The House of Osman then monopolized the trade routes from Europe to the East to amass great wealth. It reached its peak between 1520 and 1566 CE during the reign of Suleiman the Magnificent. He created a uniform legal code, and patronized arts and literature. The empire expanded to include Syria, Arabia, Palestine, Egypt, and parts of Eastern Europe (Hungary, Greece, Bulgaria and Romania).

EMPEROR SULEIMAN

3 The Renaissance and the Industrial Revolution in Europe overshadowed the Ottomans and they kept losing territory to conquests, revolts and civil wars, ceding most of their European territories during the Balkan Wars (1912–13 CE). The First World War added to this decline, with the defeat of the Ottomans. The last emperor was Mehmet VI (reign: 1918–22 CE), who was forced to abdicate after the Turkish War for Independence (1919–23 CE), led by a military leader and statesman Kemal Ataturk.

56 The House of Zhu

A family of emperors during Ming rule in China, the House of Zhu ruled from 1368 to 1644 CE.

1 During the mid-1300s, China was ruled by the Yuan dynasty, one of the Mongolian Khanates formed after Genghis Khan's death. However, the Yuans discriminated against the native Chinese. Amid famines, plagues and civil wars, a young leader, Zhu Yuanzhang, built a small army and forced the Yuans to retreat to Mongolia. Taking over as the Hongwu emperor, he established the Ming dynasty, with his descendants being known as belonging to the Zhu family. After Hongwu's death in 1398 CE, the empire passed on to his grandson, the Jianwen emperor. But Jianwen was overthrown by his uncle, the Yongle emperor, who moved the capital to Beijing, built many administrative structures and completed the construction of the Forbidden City.

2 The rule of the House of Zhu was a time of prosperity for China. The family established trade relationships with the Europeans, and started sending caravans to Europe, carrying

goods such as tea, porcelain, spices and silk. Their monopoly over trade in the region made them wealthy. The Zhus were great patrons of art and developed a style in which subtle colours were used to depict landscapes, flowers and even their emperors. The Zhu family are also known for their innovation in ceramics, and porcelain was crafted using kaolin, porcelain stone, feldspar, and quartz.

A DEPICTION OF THE FORBIDDEN CITY, INCLUDING ITS ARCHITECTS

3 By early 1600 CE, many challenges plagued the House of Zhu. Amid the financial drain due to wars with Korea and Japan, civil wars, succession battles and misrule, an uprising under Li Zincheng, a rebel peasant leader, gathered steam and led to the defeat of the Ming army in 1644. The last emperor from the House of Zhu killed all his family members and then himself. The Shun dynasty established by Li Zincheng lasted only a year, and was overthrown by the Qing dynasty.

57 The Romanov Dynasty

Comprising a long line of tsars, the Romanov dynasty ruled Russia from 1613 to 1917 CE.

1 The Romanovs take their name from Roman Yurievich, a Russian warlord whose daughter Anastasiya was the first wife of Ivan the Terrible, the first Tsar of Russia from 1547 to 1584 CE. The family was pulled into a dynastic struggle from 1598 to 1613 CE. Though exiled at first, Michael I, the 16-year-old son of the family patriarch was chosen as the ruler of Russia. He became the Tsar, the first in a line of 18 Romanovs who occupied the throne of Russia.

CROWD REQUESTING MIKHAIL ROMANOV'S MOTHER TO LET HIM BECOME THEIR TSAR

2 It was under Peter the Great (reign: 1682–1725), the grandson of Michael I, that large-scale changes took place. He modernized Russia, built it as a naval power, and introduced a new calendar and alphabet. Russia became a dominant regional power after wars with the Ottomans and Sweden. From 1762 to 1796 CE, under Catherine the Great (the wife of Karl Ulrich, the grandson of Peter the Great), Russia saw a golden age in the arts, philosophy and culture, and was integrated into Europe in terms of its outlook. Another great Romanov ruler was Alexander I (reign: 1801–25 CE), who defeated the French troops under Napoleon in 1812 CE, and weakened his campaign across Europe.

PETER THE GREAT

3 The last Romanov ruler was Tsar Nicholas II, who mishandled the Russo-Japanese War (1904–05) and, the uprising of Russian workers in 1905 CE. His rule was plagued by famines and food shortages. It set the stage for the Bolshevik Revolution led by Vladimir Lenin, which replaced Romanov rule in 1917 CE with communism.

58 The House of Medici

A wealthy Italian family based in Florence, the Medicis are credited in large measure for inspiring the Italian Renaissance. They existed from 1434 to 1737 CE.

1 The family originated in the Tuscany region of Italy and then migrated to Florence. They initially created their wealth from the textile

GIOVANNI DI BICCI DE' MEDICI, THE FOUNDER OF MEDICI BANK

trade and eventually established a bank in 1397 – the Medici Bank – which was the largest in Europe until its fall in 1494. The wealth that the Medicis generated from the bank enabled them to emerge as one of the richest families in Europe, which they used effectively to gain political power.

2 The House of Medici emerged as an influential group during the 15th century when Cosimo di Giovanni used his wealth to establish the family also as the effective rulers of Florence. As their influence increased, four popes of the Catholic Church were selected from this family – Pope Leo X, Clement VII, Pius IV and Leo XI – and there also emerged several dukes and two queens of France. The Medicis used their wealth to create an environment where art and humanism flourished. They patronized great artists and sculptors, such as Leonardo da Vinci, Michelangelo, Raphael and Botticelli, and scientists such as Galileo Galilei. The works of art they funded include legacies such as the Sistine chapel, the statue of David, the *Mona Lisa* and *The Last Supper*. They also built the St Peter's Basilica and the Santa Maria del Fiore churches. Under them, Florence emerged as the cultural centre of Europe.

3 During the latter part of their rule, the Medicis turned more authoritarian in nature. Though this change resulted in more stability in administration, it affected the growth of culture, which had earlier blossomed with individual freedom. Hence, the prominence of Florence began to fade. In 1737, when the last Medici grand duke died without a successor, the House of Medici came to an end. Their regions then passed over to the House of Habsburg, through a marriage alliance.

THE HOUSE OF MEDICI'S COAT OF ARMS, FLORENCE

59 The House of Rothschild

A wealthy Jewish family, with origins traced back to Frankfurt, Germany, founded the House of Rothschild in 1577 CE.

1 The Rothschild family began with Izaak Elchanan Rothschild, with their family name derived from the German word for 'Red Shield', a symbol displayed on the first house his family occupied. However, the family rose to prominence during the time of Mayer Amschel Rothschild, who lived from 1744 to 1812 CE. He initially did an apprenticeship at the banking firm of Oppenheimer in Hanover, where he picked up knowledge of foreign trade and currency exchange. He then started his own moneylending business along with his sons. His fortunes turned around when he was appointed as the personal supplier of coins to Prince William of Hesse-Kassel, a noble family of Germany.

MAYER AMSCHEL ROTHSCHILD

Mayer eventually came to be known as the 'founding father of international finance'.

2 Over the years, the Rothschilds' business expanded and acquired global prominence. Apart from banks all over the world, they played a critical hand in the fortunes of many rulers and governments. They raised funds to support both Britain's and Napoleon's armies during the Napoleonic Wars. In 1815, during the colonial wars, they supported Britain financially. The Japanese government sought their help for funding the Russo-Japanese war. They loaned money to the Prussian government, funded railway systems across the globe and helped the Bank of England to tide over their financial crisis. They lent Britain four million pounds to buy stocks for the Suez Canal. The Rothschild family raised capital for the independence of Brazil from Portugal and funded the creation of the African colony of Rhodesia.

3 Though the Rothschild family members have always been highly secretive about their fortunes, at the peak of their riches, the family is estimated to have owned 400 billion dollars, at par with the Mansa Musa, Emperor of the Mali Empire, who is considered as the richest

person in history. The family was elevated to the rank of nobility both by the Holy Roman Empire and the United Kingdom, and is ranked among the top most influential business houses of all time. The family owned or built more than 40 palaces, more than most royal families ever had. Currently, the Rothschilds, despite their public profile, continue to wield considerable power. Their fortunes are divided among many family members, who have gone on to support many charities and museums across the world.

HALTON HOUSE, A ROTHSCHILD MANSION IN BUCKINGHAMSHIRE, ENGLAND, IS ONE OF MANY SUCH FAMILY RESIDENCES

60 The House of Saud

A royal family originating in Saudi Arabia, the House of Saud was founded in 1720 CE.

1 The House of Saud emerged in 1447 CE, when Mani Ibn Rabiah from an ancient Arab tribe, was gifted a few estates by his relative ibn Dir, a ruler of Riyadh. Their clan eventually grew larger. Around 1744 CE, Muhammad Ibn Saud, their chief, withstood attacks of the Ottoman Empire and conquered most of modern-day Saudi Arabia, including the holy cities of Mecca and Medina. Though they were defeated by the Ottomans in 1818 CE, Ibn Saud's grandson Turki made a comeback and won back his territories in 1824 CE, reinstating the Saudi state for a second time. It was rather short-lived, though, because of internal civil wars and the family fled to Kuwait. Later in 1902 CE, the Saud family, under the leadership of Abdulaziz bin Abdul Rahman Al Saud, known popularly as ibn Saud, with the help of arms supplied by the Kuwaiti Emir, managed to capture and unite their kingdom again, and then established the kingdom of Saudi Arabia.

2 The head of the House of Saud holds the position of the head of state in the kingdom of Saudi Arabia and is also referred to as the 'Custodian of the two holy mosques of Mecca and Medina'. The key ministries in the state, including defence, internal affairs and foreign affairs, are held by members of the family. The House of Saud, with their ownership of Saudi Aramco, a crude oil firm and one of the largest enterprises in the world in terms of revenue, is currently the wealthiest family in the world.

ABDULAZIZ BIN ABDUL RAHMAN AL SAUD (IBN SAUD)

3 The current ruler of Saudi Arabia is Salman bin Abdulaziz, who ascended the throne in 2015. Though, immediately after taking over, he had named his nephew Mohammed bin Nayef as the heir to the throne, Bin Nayef was relieved in 2017 and replaced by Mohammed bin Salman, the son of the current ruler.

61 The House of Windsor

The current ruling royal family in the United Kingdom, the House of Windsor was established in 1917 CE by King George V.

1 Monarchs from the House of Hanover ruled the United Kingdom (UK) from the 17th to the 20th century. Queen Victoria, the last monarch from the House of Hanover, was married to Prince Albert of the House of Saxe-Coburg and Gotha, an influential aristocratic family connected to most European ruling families. Victoria was succeeded by Edward VII, her eldest son, the first British monarch from the House of Saxe-Coburg and Gotha in 1901, replacing the House of Hanover. He was succeeded by George V, who on 19 June 1917 ordered all German names and surnames to be changed, due to the ongoing First World War against the Germans. So his

KING EDWARD VII

own family name was changed from Saxe-Coburg and Gotha to Windsor. The Windsors follow the Magna Carta, signed in 1215 CE by their ancestor King John, which places the monarch as a symbolic leader; political decisions are the parliament's.

2 The Windsors belong to a period when most British colonies, such as, Zambia, Egypt and Malaysia, gained freedom after India's independence in 1947. However, the British monarch is still the head of state of 15 sovereign states besides the UK, including Canada, Australia and New Zealand. The Windsors are known for their role in wars: King George V and Queen Mary visited front-line trenches, while their son George VI, served in the navy during the First World War. Queen Elizabeth II, the current monarch, is honorary colonel of the Grenadier Guards, the most senior of five regiments. She is also one of the longest ruling monarchs in the world.

3 The Windsors have been in the eye of many controversies. These include Prince Charles, the heir apparent to the British throne, divorcing Princess Diana, and more recently, Prince Harry, their son, and his wife Meghan Markle, stepping down as senior members of the royal family.

ARTISTS AND ARCHITECTS

62 Leonardo da Vinci

A Renaissance-period painter, Leonardo da Vinci was a sculptor and inventor who lived from 1452 to 1519 CE in Florence, Italy.

1 Da Vinci was born in Tuscany, Italy, and received no formal education as a child until he was apprenticed at the age of 15 under the noted painter Andrea del Verrocchio, from whom he learnt

LEONARDO DA VINCI, A PORTRAIT

to refine his techniques. Da Vinci's first independent commission was for an altarpiece inside Florence's Palazzo Vecchio. Da Vinci learnt and perfected a special style of art called the sfumato, softening the transition between colours with curved and realistic sketches rather than straight and perfect ones.

2 Da Vinci's most famous works include the *The Last Supper*, commissioned by the Duke of Milan, which took three years to complete. In 1503, he started working on the *Mona Lisa*, a privately commissioned portrait of a woman characterized by her enigmatic smile, using his famous sfumato technique. His other famous works included *The Virgin of the Rocks*, *Lady with an Ermine*, *The Vitruvian Man* and *Salvator Mundi*.

3 Da Vinci took a deep interest in a range of subjects including fine art, nature, mechanics, anatomy, physics, architecture and weaponry. He tested scientific laws, dissected bodies and wrote down detailed observations on mainly four broad themes: painting, architecture, mechanics and anatomy. He has to his credit the creation of workable designs for the bicycle, helicopter, submarine and military tank. During the final years of his life, Da Vinci entered into the service

of the French king, leaving Italy forever. Here he spent most of his time in scientific research and documentation. He died while he was in France.

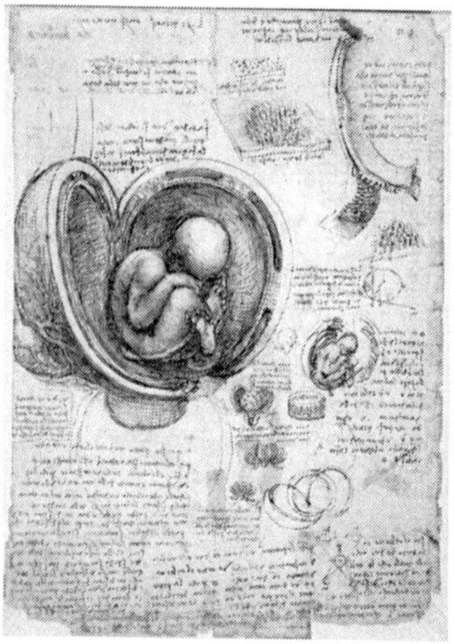

LEONARDO'S STUDY OF A FOETUS IN THE WOMB AND THE *MONA LISA* (HIS MOST FAMOUS PAINTING)

63 Michelangelo Buonarroti

A Renaissance sculptor, Michelangelo Buonarroti was also an artist and an architect, who lived from 1465 to 1564 CE. He is considered as one of the greatest artists of all time and his work exerted a great influence on the future of Western art.

1 Michelangelo was born in the village of Caprese in Tuscany, Italy, as the second son of a government administrator. At the age of thirteen, he became an apprentice to a famous painter, Domenico Ghirlandaio, In whose studio he was exposed to the technique of fresco. From there, he was patronized by Lorenzo Medici, the ruler of Florence, to study classical sculpture. He also obtained special permission from the Catholic Church to study cadavers for insight into the human anatomy, which later helped him develop a distinct style of muscular precision.

MICHELANGELO, A PORTRAIT

2 After Medici's death in 1498, Michelangelo moved to Rome, where he was commissioned to do the 'Pieta', a sculpture of Mother Mary holding the dead Jesus across her lap, from a single piece of marble. Then he undertook 'David', a 17-feet statue. Pope Julius II commissioned Michelangelo to decorate the 5,000-square-foot ceiling of the Sistine Chapel, which he completed all alone! His other famous works include *Moses, Madonna on the Steps, Madonna and Child* and *Doni Tondo*.

THE CREATION OF ADAM BY MICHELANGELO, FROM THE SISTINE CHAPEL IN ROME

3 Michelangelo produced numerous other sculptures, frescoes, architectural designs, and drawings. An accomplished poet, he left behind nearly 300 poems. He is now regarded as a giant of the Florentine High Renaissance. He died in Rome, leaving his last sculpture incomplete.

64 Mimar Sinan

Ottaman architect par excellence, Mimar Sinan lived from 1489 to 1588 CE. His ideas shaped not only Ottoman architecture, but also the Islamic design aesthetic across the world and across ages.

1 During his youth, Sinan helped his father, a stone mason and carpenter. He started out as an architect in Cairo, assisting in the construction of defences and bridges, and converting churches in

MIMAR SINAN (POSSIBLY FAR LEFT) OVERSEEING THE CONSTRUCTION OF OTTOMAN RULER SULEIMAN'S TOMB

captured territories into mosques. By 1539, he took charge as the Architect of the Ottoman Empire. Influenced by the Byzantine-built Hagia Sophia in Istanbul, he adopted the same square base with a dome on top of it and added his own elements.

2 Sinan completed almost 370 works including 150 mosques, 36 palaces, 48 public baths, 20 mausoleums and 10 bridges across Istanbul, Edirne, Ankara, Kayseri, Aleppo, Damascus and Buda. His masterwork, the Selimiye Mosque, is said to have the 'perfect' dome. His unique 'unit circle method' made buildings earthquake-proof: his Suleymaniye Complex has withstood over 100 earthquakes in Istanbul.

THE INTERIOR OF THE SULEYMANIYE MOSQUE

3 Sinan's leading works in Istanbul included the İbrahim Pasha Palace, and the minarets of the Hagia Sophia Mosque. Called 'Koca' (Great), he became even more famous when Mughal emperor Shah Jahan used his architectural style for the Taj Mahal.

65 Rembrandt van Rijn

A Dutch painter and printmaker, Rembrandt van Rijn lived from 1606 to 1669 CE. He was known for using realism, and light and shade.

1 Rembrandt dropped out of a Latin school to be trained as an artist. He took two masters: the first one for the basics, and the second one, Pieter Lastman, for insight into historical paintings. his art. He also devoted himself to an intense study of people, objects and their surroundings.

REMBRANDT, A SELF-PORTRAIT

2 Following the Protestant Reformation, churches did not commission any art, and Rembrandt had to seek private commissions. So, initially, he devoted himself to small-scale historical paintings. He then moved to Amsterdam, growing into a prominent portraitist. He went on to become highly successful, and his most important works included *The Anatomy Lesson of Dr Nicolaes Tulp*, *Self-Portrait*, *Aristotle with a Bust of Homer* and *The Night Watch*, a fine example of how Rembrandt used light and darkness.

3 Rembrandt is noted for his remarkable ability to express human emotions through his artwork. He inspired numerous artists, including modern ones like Edward Hopper, Frank Auerback and Francis Bacon.

THE NIGHT WATCH (LEFT) AND *THE THREE TREES*

66 Christopher Wren

One of the most acclaimed English architects in history, Christopher Wren is also well known for his skills in designing, geometry and astronomy. He lived from 1632 to 1723 CE.

1 Wren was born to the Dean of Windsor in England and developed an interest in mathematics and astronomy from the intellectuals in the king's court. He was educated at the University of Oxford and then took up a job as a professor of astronomy, initially at Gresham College, London, and then at Oxford.

SIR CHRISTOPHER WREN, A PORTRAIT

2 In 1662, when Wren was engaged for designing the Sheldonian Theatre at Oxford, a gift of Bishop Gilbert Sheldon to the University of Oxford, his main interest turned to architecture. Bishop Sheldon also started discussing with Wren the restoration of St Paul's Cathedral,

London. In 1665, Wren visited Paris, where he was strongly influenced by the French baroque style. After the Great Fire of London, Wren relocated to London, where he eventually took charge as the king's surveyor of works, with the responsibility of rebuilding 52 churches in the City of London.

3 St Paul's Cathedral, which took nearly 35 years to build, is regarded as Wren's masterpiece. Other notable buildings designed by Wren included the Royal Observatory, the Royal Naval College, the College of Physicians, the Chelsea Hospital and the Trinity College Library in Cambridge. When Christopher Wren died in 1723, he became the first person to be buried in St Paul's Cathedral.

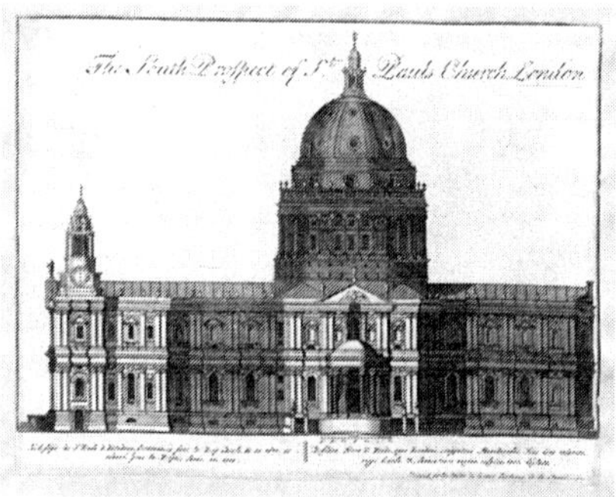

ST PAUL'S CATHEDRAL, AN ETCHING

67 Claude Monet

A French artist who is considered as the founder of the Impressionist style of art, Claude Monet lived from 1840 to 1926 CE.

1 Monet was born in Rue Laffitte, Paris, to a grocer, and spent his childhood along beaches in Normandy, gaining intimate knowledge about nature, the sea and changing weather conditions. During the initial part of his career, Monet was introduced to landscape paintings by Eugene Boudin, an artist who taught him to paint in natural and outdoor settings rather than inside studios.

CLAUDE MONET, A PORTRAIT

2 Monet eventually settled in Giverny, west of Paris, in the region of Normandy, and began to develop his own technique. He captured the essence of the natural world using strong colours and bold, short brushstrokes. Critics started

to refer to his work as 'impressionism', suggesting that his work seemed more like sketches than finished paintings. Monet also painted things in a series, trying to convey a certain time of day or a season in a landscape or a place. His famous works included *Water Lilies*, *Haystacks*, *Poplars*, the 'London Parliament' series and the 'Sunrise Rouen Cathedral' series.

3 Claude Monet helped change the world of art by shaking off the previously held ornate and inaccessible conventions, and establishing a new movement in art. He influenced several great artists including Vincent van Gogh. Towards the end of his life, Monet started to develop cataract, which affected his perception of colour. He became more reclusive in nature and his output reduced drastically.

IMPRESSION, SUNRISE

68 Vincent van Gogh

A Dutch artist, Vincent van Gogh was considered as the greatest of the post-Impressionists. He lived from 1853 to 1890 CE.

1 Van Gogh was the child of a Protestant pastor and lived in southern Netherlands. At the age of sixteen, he started working with an art dealer in London and then in Paris, where he developed a taste for art. He then took up a job as a missionary serving the poor. This period had a deep influence on him as he was exposed to the sufferings of the underserved. Van Gogh then started looking at art as a tool that could provide hope to the poor.

VAN GOGH, A SELF-PORTRAIT

2 He worked as an artist for a short period, only a decade from 1880 until 1890 CE. During the initial years, he worked under a Dutch landscape artist, developing a perspective and liking for nature. Van Gogh then moved to the countryside to spend time with peasants, where he started to

realize larger possibilities for his paintings. In 1886, he moved to Paris and started experimenting with a unique style using spontaneity, bright colours, light tonalities and broken brushwork, in a total divergence from traditional techniques, thereby developing a post-Impressionist style. During the last year of his life, he suffered from a mental illness and had to be institutionalized. He painted one of his most famous works, *The Starry Night,* out of his memory of what the outside world looked like. Once he was out of confinement, he shot himself and died two days later.

3 During his short career and life, Vincent van Gogh completed more than 2,000 works, consisting of more than 800 oil paintings and 1,300 watercolours and sketches. Several of his paintings now rank among the most expensive in the world. His famous works include *The Potato Eaters*, *The Bedroom*, *Wheatfield with Crows* and *Sunflowers*.

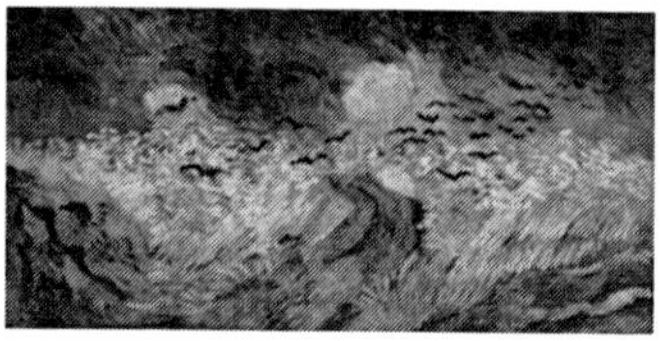

WHEATFIELD WITH CROWS

69

Antoni Gaudi

A famous architect who lived in Spain from 1852 to 1926 CE, Antoni Gaudi is regarded as one of the leading exponents of modernism.

1 Gaudi was born in a family of coppersmiths, who made boilers. As he worked in his family workshop, he acquired skills of conceptualizing in three dimensions, designing spaces and transforming materials. He took a deep interest in studying patterns embedded in nature and how these could be translated while designing spaces. During his initial years, Gaudi was fascinated by organic architecture, a way of merging the natural world with human habitat.

ANTONI GAUDI,
A PORTRAIT

2 In 1870, Gaudi moved to Barcelona to study architecture. However, being an inconsistent student, he took eight years to complete his degree. Upon graduation, though he initially worked

on some Victorian styles, he soon developed a personal style of his own, using juxtapositions of geometric patterns with bricks, stones, bright ceramic tiles and metals. He also experimented with various historic styles including the Gothic and the Baroque. In the latter half, Gaudi created a type of structure called 'equilibrated', which could stand on its own without internal or external bracings. During his final years, Gaudi focused entirely on Sagrada Familia, a large Roman Catholic minor basilica, which remains unfinished.

3 Gaudi is regarded as the inventor of a unique and incomparable architectural language, and sometimes even regarded as being eccentric. His most famous works include the Bellesguard Tower, the Park Güell, the Casa Milà, El Capricho de Gaudí, the Casa Batlló, La Pedrera and the Church of the Sagrada Familia in Spain. He died in a street accident.

SIGNATURE GAUDI-STYLE ARCHITECTURE IN BARCELONA, SPAIN

70 Louis Henry Sullivan

An American architect who lived from 1856 to 1924 CE, Louis Henry Sullivan is regarded as the spiritual father of modern American architecture, and is called 'the father of skyscrapers'.

1 Sullivan studied at the Massachusetts Institute of Technology's architectural programme, which he left after a year for an apprenticeship. Initially working in Chicago, he went to Europe, only to return to Chicago. Along with architect and civil engineer Dankmar Adler, he started a firm, Adler and Sullivan Architects. In their 14-year association, they built more than 100 buildings, many of them landmarks in American and world architecture.

LOUIS HENRY SULLIVAN

2 The first major building he designed was in 1886 CE: the 'Auditorium building', a hotel and office in a 'U' shape around an auditorium. Sullivan designed around 40 buildings between 1890 and 1895 CE, which included

the Wainwright Building, the first tall building to celebrate verticality. Sullivan emphasized the vertical form of buildings, a principle that led to the coinage of the 'form follows function' axiom.

3 Sullivan rejected the popular style during his day, drawn from classical Greek and Roman styles, and developed the unique 'Chicago school of architecture', employing steel framed buildings clad in ornamental masonry, which influenced modernist architects. Among his famous buildings are the Wainwright Building, the Guaranty Building and the Getty Tomb.

THE PRUDENTIAL (OR GUARANTY) BUILDING IN BUFFALO, NEW YORK – A HERITAGE SKYSCRAPER

71 Le Corbusier

Charles-Édouard Jeanneret, popularly known as Le Corbusier, was an internationally acclaimed Swiss-French architect and city planner, regarded as the pioneer of modern architecture. He lived from 1885 to 1965 CE.

1 Le Corbusier was born in La Chaux-de-Fonds in a mountainous Swiss region. In his formative years, he learnt art history and drawing. After his studies, he undertook a series of trips across Europe and the Mediterranean to self-train as an architect.

2 At thirty, he returned to Paris and was introduced to Purism, an art form celebrating the pure, simple geometric forms of everyday objects. In 1922 CE, he started a studio with his cousin and developed his famous 'five points of architecture'. They were: (i) pilotis or the lifting of a building over pilots; (ii) the free designing of the ground plan; (iii) the free design of the façade; (iv) the horizontal window; and (v) roof gardens or green roofs. He published his most important work, *Towards a New Architecture*, a book that contained

his vision for modern architecture and smooth machine-like houses. During the second phase of his career, he developed a different style, favouring exposed concrete and monumental size, now known as Brutalism.

LE CORBUSIER

3 Le Corbusier had a great influence on modern architecture and urban planning. His most famous buildings include the Viila Savoye, the chapel of Notre Dame du Haut in Ronchamp and the Carpenter Centre for the Visual Arts. His master plan of Chandigarh, India, was a grand project at the invitation of the then Indian prime minister, Jawaharlal Nehru, and buildings like the Palace of Assembly here stand testimony to his unique aesthetic.

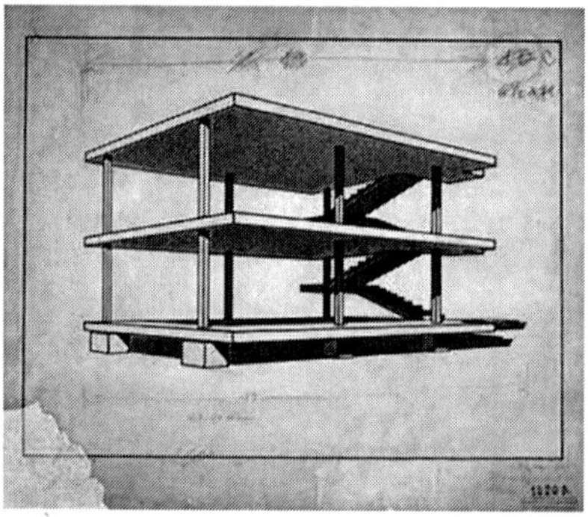

MAISON DOM-INO (DOM-INO HOUSE), 1914–15

72 Pablo Picasso

One of the most influential artists in history, Pablo Picasso lived from 1881 to 1973 CE. He was one of the main creators of the Cubism art movement.

1 Picasso's father was a professor of drawing and Picasso joined a local art academy in Barcelona to graduate as an academic painter. However, soon he broke away from art school training. During a stint in Paris, he started deviating from the orthodox Spanish monochromatic palette of blacks and browns and moved on to experimenting with bright colours using pastels, watercolours and oils.

PABLO PICASSO

2 Picasso's works are divided into several periods, such as the 'Blue' period (1901–04 CE) with beggars, mothers and children as subjects in blue-green shades; the 'Rose' period (1904–06 CE), with circus characters in orange and pink tones characters. From 1907 to 1909 CE, he was influenced by African artefacts and

primitivism. Then, with his friend Georges Braque, he developed a unique style called Analytic Cubism, showing objects as shapes in monochrome shades. His Cubist paintings gave him fame and fortune. In his final years, he painted his masterwork, *Guernica*, depicting people's suffering and his hope for peace during the Spanish civil war.

3 He produced more than 50,000 artworks, the most famous being *Les Demoiselles d'Avignon*, *The Old Guitarist*, *Girl before a Mirror* and *Portrait of Gertrude Stein*. He influenced later great artists like Juan Gris and Paul Cezanne.

PIERROT, PAINTED BY PICASSO IN PARIS, 1918

POETS, MUSICIANS AND AUTHORS

73 Homer

Homer was an ancient Greek poet, believed to be one of the greatest, who lived around the eighth century BCE in Ionia.

1 While there are no clear records of the life of Homer, and we know very little about his personal life, historians think he was visually impaired. He was dubbed as 'the teacher of all of Greece' by Plato.

2 Homer is credited with composing two epic poems – *The Iliad* and *The Odyssey*. *The Iliad* is divided into 24 books, corresponding to each letter of the Greek alphabet, beginning with alpha and ending at omega. This book narrated the final year of the Trojan War, fought between the Greeks and the defenders of the city of Troy, also called Ilium. *The Odyssey* is set in a period after the Trojan War, which had been won by the Greeks. It spoke about the journey of the Greek hero Odysseus and the troubles he faced in his times.

3 Homer's epics laid the foundation for ancient Greek culture and later contributed towards the rise of Roman culture. *The Odyssey* is considered to be the foundation of Humanism, which engendered the development of all kinds of arts and sciences in Western culture.

A DEPICTION OF HOMER (CENTRE) WITH DANTE AND VIRGIL

74 Sophocles

Sophocles was one of the most celebrated and greatest of ancient Greek playwrights. He lived from 496 to 406 BCE.

1 Sophocles was born in a village outside Athens to a wealthy family and received a great education during his formative years. He was an eminent writer and was chosen to lead the paean (a choral chant to a god), celebrating the Greek victory over the Persians at the Battle of Salamis fought between an alliance of Greek city states under Themistocles, and the Persian Empire led by King Xerxes.

2 Sophocles was an innovative playwright, adding a third actor in a scene that had previously transpired only between two. This created realistic action and deeper development of characters. In all, he wrote around 120 plays, out of which the major ones included *Ajax*, *Oedipus the King* and *Electra*. His plays dramatized stories in the most tragic manner.

3 During his time, Sophocles was the most celebrated playwright in Greek theatre competitions for almost 50 years. He won the first prize at the 'Great Dionysia', a drama festival, close to 18 times. Sophocles has endured as a dramatist and his works are studied even to this day. He died at the age of 90, where his last public act was leading a chorus at a public mourning of one of his contemporary playwrights, Euripides.

PORTRAIT OF THE GREEK ACTOR EUIAON IN SOPHOCLES'S *ANDROMEDA*

75 Thiruvalluvar

Thiruvalluvar was an Indian philosopher and poet, who lived in Tamil Nadu. His birth year is assumed to be around the first century BCE.

1 Thiruvalluvar was born in Tamil Nadu, India. He came from a humble background. Little is known about his early life. It is still a matter of debate if Thiruvalluvar was a Hindu or a Jain, owing to his views on non-violence.

2 Thiruvalluvar wrote the *Tirukkural*, considered a masterpiece on human behaviour and conduct in society at large. It contains 1,330 couplets divided among 133 sections. The book is divided into three parts, each part covering important teachings on virtue, wealth and love. Out of this, the second part is the longest, which talks about morality, ethics and conduct with respect to statecraft, politics and warfare. Many scholars compare *Tirukkural* to other classic texts, such as Confucian sayings, John Milton's *Paradise Lost* and even the Bible.

THIRUVALLUVAR, AN ARTIST'S IMPRESSION

3 Thiruvalluvar is also considered by many as the greatest poet of south India. He is believed to be a saint and is worshipped by some communities. In the 16th century, a temple was built and dedicated to him in the Mylapore region of Chennai, India.

76

Virgil

A Classical-Era Roman poet who lived from 70 BCE to 19 BCE, Virgil grew up in tumultuous times when the Roman Republic was coming to an end.

1 Virgil was born in a village in Italy. He was educated in Rome, where one of his teachers was an Epicurean philosopher called Siro. This influence is visible in some of his work. Virgil was also affected by the series of civil wars that occurred during the time of Julius Caesar.

A FIFTH-CENTURY PORTRAIT OF VIRGIL FROM THE *VERGILIUS ROMANUS*

2 Virgil's first major work was the *Eclogues*, inspired by Homer, reflecting the tragedies of his times. This was followed by *Georgics*. During the last few years of his life, Virgil worked on the *Aeneid*, considered as the national epic of ancient Rome. The

Aeneid followed the struggles of a Trojan warrior named Aeneas, whose descendants eventually founded the city of Rome.

3 Virgil's work greatly influenced future Western literature in structure and style. Mainly during the Renaissance period, many authors were inspired by Virgil's works. He is thought to have died of fever while sailing with the purpose of editing the *Aeneid*. The work is thought to have been left incomplete and unedited.

77 Kalidasa

One of the greatest authors and playwright on the Indian subcontinent, Kalidasa lived during the fifth century CE.

1 Kalidasa is believed to have belonged to a Hindu family in north or central India. Some historians suggest that he could have been a member of the court of Chandragupta II of the Gupta dynasty, who ruled between 380 and 415 CE. The reign of Chandragupta II is considered the golden period for Indian cultural development, where art, architecture, sculpture and literature reached their zenith.

2 Kalidasa's famous play *Abhijnana Shakuntalam*, well noted for its description of nature and elegant metaphors, talks about the relationship between Shankutala, the daughter of sage Vishwamitra, and King Dushyanta, and their child Bharata who is believed to have laid the foundation of India as a nation. His other works include the play *Vikramorvashi*, epic poem *Raghuvamsha* and lyric poem *Meghaduta*.

3 Kalidasa's works helped synthesize Brahminic traditions to a more secular form of Hinduism, which was gaining a foothold during the reign of Chandragupta II. Kalidasa's contributions are considered significant in ushering in the golden age of Indian literature.

KALIDASA, AN ARTIST'S IMPRESSION

78 Rumi

Rumi is the greatest of all Sufi poets, and is said to have had a lasting impact on Islamic literature. He lived from 1207 to 1273 CE.

1 Rumi was born in the Balkh province of present-day Afghanistan, which was at that time a part of the Persian Empire. When he was young, his family was forced to flee, as Genghis Khan planned his invasion of the region. They eventually settled in Turkey.

2 In 1244, Rumi met Shams, a wandering holy man; this was a defining moment in his life. They formed a close bond, but in four years, Shams was either driven away or killed, which left a huge void in Rumi's life. Rumi composed more than 40,000 lyrical verses, as an outpouring over the loss of his friend; this resulted in the *Diwan-e-Shams-e Tabrizi*, considered one of the greatest works of Persian literature. In the latter part of his life, Rumi connected with another friend, Chelebi, who eventually became his deputy. He composed his main work *Masnavi-yi Ma'navi*,

his masterpiece, under this new friend's influence. Many Sufis consider this work as the most important work in the Persian language.

3 Rumi's works have influenced poets and philosophers across the Islamic world and as far as in Greece, Central Asia and the Indian subcontinent. His poems have been translated into many languages and he is regarded amongst the most relevant poets delving into the themes of mysticism, spiritual love, yearning and joy. Rumi's death in 1273 CE after falling ill was mourned by all communities including Jews and Christians.

RUMI, AN ARTIST'S IMPRESSION

79 William Shakespeare

Considered among the greatest writers and poets in world history, William Shakespeare lived from 1564 to 1616 CE in England.

1 William Shakespeare was born in Stratford-upon-Avon, Warwickshire, where he attended the local grammar school and learnt Latin. Shakespeare was just 18 years old when he got married, and between his twins' baptism in 1585 and his appearance on the London theatre scene in 1592, there is no record of his life – these are known as the 'lost years'.

WILLIAM SHAKESPEARE

2 By 1592 CE, Shakespeare started as a playwright in London. Over the course of the next two decades, until 1613 CE, he wrote a total of 38 plays, many of them historical ones, such as *Henry VI*, *Richard II*, *Henry V* and Julius

Caesar. He also wrote comedies, such as *The Merchant of Venice* and *A Midsummer Night's Dream*. In the latter period, he wrote tragedies such as: *Hamlet, Othello, King Lear* and *Macbeth*. In 1599, Shakespeare built his own theatre on the bank of the River Thames, called the Globe Theatre.

3 Shakespeare's works have had a long-lasting influence on language, theatre and literature. He introduced many new words into the English language. His use of language helped shape modern English grammar, spelling and pronunciation. In his final years, Shakespeare is thought to have retired to Stratford, a time during which the bubonic plague was devastating London. During this period, he wrote fewer plays. He died in 1616, following a period of illness.

PROCESSION OF CHARACTERS FROM SHAKESPEARE'S PLAYS

80 John Milton

Thought to be one of the greatest English poets, John Milton lived in England from 1608 to 1674 CE.

1 Milton was born to a composer in London. He went to the University of Cambridge, after which he spent the next six years preparing for a career as a poet. Milton gained proficiency in Latin, Greek and Italian during this period.

2 During the English civil war, Milton wrote several articles advocating for radical political topics. After the war, by 1652 CE, Milton lost his eyesight owing to an unknown illness; however, he continued his work by dictating to a scribe. After the restoration of the monarchy in 1660 CE, Milton was arrested. Though he was released later, he lived the rest of his life in seclusion, completing his magnum opus, *Paradise Lost*, and its sequel, *Paradise Regained*.

JOHN MILTON

Paradise Lost narrates the story of Adam and Eve losing paradise, and it is regarded as one of the foremost epic poems in world literature.

3 Milton's works inspired many other great poets who came after him, such as William Wordsworth and William Blake. Many historians consider him as the most significant English author after William Shakespeare. He died possibly of tuberculosis.

A DEPICTION OF MILTON DICTATING *PARADISE LOST* TO HIS DAUGHTERS, C. 1826

81 Ludwig van Beethoven

Regarded as the most admirable composer of all time, especially in the history of Western music, Beethoven lived from 1770 to 1827 CE in Germany.

1 Beethoven was born to a family of musicians. His grandfather and godfather were eminent musicians, and his father was a musician as well. He gave Beethoven his early lessons and instilled in him the kind of dedication needed to be an excellent performer, although at times he tended to be harsh on the young Beethoven.

2 At the age of ten, Beethoven started to study music full-time with Christian Gottlob Neefe, a renowned teacher who first recognized Beethoven's musical genius. Under him Beethoven published his first composition. In 1792, as the French Revolution was brewing, Beethoven moved to Vienna and made his first public appearance as a pianist at the age of twenty-five. He undertook several concert tours and, in 1800 CE, launched his Symphony No. 1 in C Major at the Royal Imperial Theatre in Vienna. His fame soon spread across

Europe, but unfortunately, he started to develop a hearing impairment. He also had a short-lived association with the theatre, for which he composed *The Creatures of Prometheus*, a popular ballet. From 1803 CE onwards, known as the 'heroic' period in his life, he composed several symphonies, sonatas and songs, the most famous ones being the Moonlight Sonata, and Symphonies No. 3 to 8.

BEETHOVEN

3 Beethoven raised the status of instrumental music, which, until then, was considered inferior to vocals. His compositions are now

appreciated for their intensity and their perfection in design. During his final year, Beethoven fell sick with symptoms of jaundice and liver damage, and later died due to cirrhosis of the liver.

BEETHOVEN'S FUNERAL

82 Victor Hugo

One of the most enduring French novelists and poets, Victor Hugo lived from 1802 to 1885 CE.

1 Hugo was born in France, where his father was a general who served under Napoleon Bonaparte. He studied law initially but embarked on a career in literature.

2 Hugo published his first work, a novel titled *Han d'Islande*, in 1823. About eight years later, he published *The Hunchback of Notre Dame*, which condemned society, deeming it unjust and seeking to rid it of its inhibitions. After the success of this work, Hugo started to plan another major work around the misery and injustice of his time. Ultimately in 1862 CE, Les Misérables was published, and became an immediate success in Europe and the United States of America. However, Hugo suffered several tragedies in

VICTOR HUGO

his later life, including a period of exile and the loss of his sons. This began reflecting in his later work, which began to reveal darker shades in his psyche. He died of a stroke.

3 Victor Hugo had a profound influence on many political and social issues of his time. His literary achievements and undying optimism in human progress established him somewhat as a national hero.

COSETTE SWEEPING.

ILLUSTRATION BY ÉMILE BAYARD FROM THE ORIGINAL EDITION OF *LES MISÉRABLES* (1862)

83 Charles Dickens

Regarded as one of the greatest novelists, Charles Dickens wrote some of the world's best known works of fiction. He lived from 1812 to 1870 CE.

1 Dickens was born in a poor family in Portsmouth, England. When he was just 12 years old, his father was imprisoned, and Dickens started working in a boot-blacking factory. Later, he worked as a freelance reporter, which opened up many opportunities for him to try his hand at writing.

CHARLES DICKENS

2 In 1836 CE, he began to gain success with the serial publication of *The Pickwick Papers*. He perfected the technique of episodic writing, keeping the readers in suspense, and at the same time allowing him to develop his characters and plots based on reader feedback. He published 15 novels

during his lifetime, including famous ones such as *Oliver Twist*, *A Christmas Carol*, *David Copperfield*, *A Tale of Two Cities* and *Great Expectations*.

3 Charles Dickens is even now one of the most read and acclaimed English authors of all time, often compared to Shakespeare. His novels have been continuously adapted to all formats, including theatre, television and cinema.

SPECTATORS BUYING TICKETS FOR A READING BY CHARLES DICKENS AT STEINWAY HALL, NEW YORK, 1867

84

Leo Tolstoy

Leo Tolstoy was a Russian author, considered among the world's enduring writers. He lived from 1828 to 1910 CE.

1 Tolstoy was born in a Russian aristocratic family. His parents died when he was a child, and he was then taken in by his relatives. He tried studying law, but left the university and started pursuing writing. He also served a stint in the army, where he fought in the Crimean War in 1855, which had an influence on some of his works. His first work was an autobiographical sketch called 'Childhood', followed by another one titled 'Boyhood'.

2 Once the Crimean War ended, Tolstoy left the army to start focusing on his literary career. In the 1860s, Tolstoy wrote his first great novel, *War and Peace*, a historical narration of the Napoleonic Wars through fictional characters. Following the success of this novel, during the next decade, Tolstoy worked on his next novel, *Anna Karenina*, which again went on to be a huge success. However, he soon felt himself embroiled

in a moral crisis, which ushered in his subsequent spiritual awakening.

3 Tolstoy's novels are considered among the best in the literary world, so much so that *War and Peace* is often cited as the greatest novel ever written, noted for its realistic detailing and deep psychological analysis of human emotions. During his final years, his health deteriorated steadily. He died of pneumonia at a railway station, while travelling.

LEO TOLSTOY

SCIENTISTS AND INVENTIONS

85

Sushruta

Known as the 'father of plastic surgery', Sushruta was a physician who lived around 600 BCE in India.

1 Sushruta practised Ayurveda, regarded as an alternative form of healing, and its origins can be traced back to 1500 BCE. According to Sushruta, diseases are caused by imbalances in the body, and the physician's duty is to identify and correct these imbalances. He believed that good health could be achieved through the harmony of the mind and the body.

2 Sushruta wrote his treatise called the *Sushruta Samhita*, an instruction manual for physicians to treat patients in a holistic manner. This treatise listed thousands of illnesses, treatments, applications of medicinal herbs, surgical procedures and even surgical instruments. Sushruta had a thorough knowledge of the human anatomy and he described procedures for several types of surgeries, such as plastic surgery, tooth extraction, treatment of internal wounds and cesarean-section births.

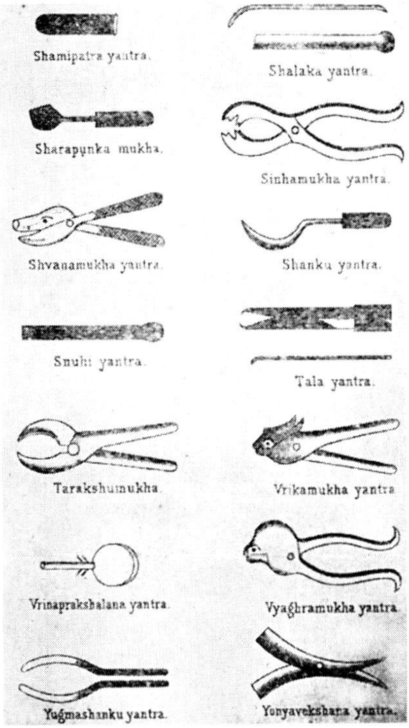

SURGICAL INSTRUMENTS MENTIONED IN THE *SUSHRUTA SAMHITA*

3 The Sushruta Samhita was translated into Arabic by Caliph Mansur in the eighth century after which it became popular in the Islamic world as well. However, the Western world took much longer, till around the early 1900s, to discover the ancient expertise of Sushruta.

86 Hippocrates

An ancient Greek physician who lived on the island of Cos in Greece from 460 to 375 BCE, Hippocrates is often referred to as the 'father of medicine'.

1 The early life of Hippocrates was recorded by Soranus, a second century CE Greek physician, who suggested that Hippocrates had acquired early knowledge of medicine from his father and grandfather. Hippocrates's works were also recorded by his contemporary philosopher, Plato, who referred to him as a well-known physician who had a philosophical approach towards medicine. Hippocrates travelled across Greece and Asia Minor, practising and teaching medicine.

2 During his time, it was believed that diseases were punishments inflicted by gods. However, Hippocrates believed that diseases were caused by natural reasons and physiological imbalances, such as diet, and living and environmental conditions, and he separated the discipline of medicine from superstitions and religion. He gave importance to observations and

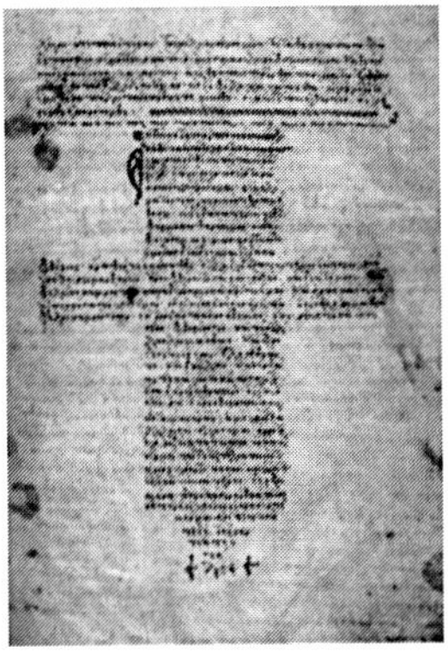

THE HIPPOCRATIC OATH, SHAPED AS A CROSS IN BYZANTINE TIMES

documentation, where physicians were asked to record their findings and medicinal methods in a clear and objective manner. The Hippocratic Oath, which laid the foundation of ethics and morals in the field of medicine, is attributed to Hippocrates.

3 Now, much of what we know about what Hippocrates believed and practised comes from 'The Hippocratic Corpus', a collection of around 70 medical works, containing texts, lectures, research findings and essays. His work revolutionized the practice of medicine. Even today, the ethical and moral aspects of the medical field are based on the Hippocratic Oath.

87 Paper

A lasting invention, paper has revolutionized human history in many ways.

1 In ancient China, documents were written on bamboo or silk. Paper fragments were recovered from a tomb in Gansu in north-west China, dating to the second century BCE, and hence an early form of paper was probably invented then. However, a Han dynasty court official, Cai Lun, is credited as the inventor of paper. He refined its recipe and production process in 105 CE. Paper was so important that this invention was a top secret in Chinese imperial courts.

2 Historians believe that the Abbasid Caliphate, an Islamic empire, procured paper-making technology when they defeated the Tang dynasty in 751 CE and captured a few Chinese prisoners who knew about it. The Abbasids created a network of paper mills across their empire, extending from the China border to north-west Africa. Paper enabled scholars to write manuscripts easily and preserve classical works by translating

them. This helped to usher in the Islamic golden age of cultural and scientific advancement, from 750 to 1258 CE. Paper was introduced on the Indian subcontinent by Buddhist pilgrims via the Silk Road. In Europe, it came to the Caliphate-ruled province of Iberia, and spread to other parts from the 10th century onwards, as Sicily and Spain came under Islamic domination. Around 1450, Johannes Gutenberg in Germany invented metal movable-type printing and revolutionized not only the use of paper but also history, by accelerating the onset of the European Renaissance, the Reformation and the Scientific Revolution.

DEPICTION OF PAPER-MAKING IN CHINA, 1637

3 In 1799, the Fourdrinier machine was invented in France, enabling mass production of paper rolls. It was powered by steam machinery, an invention of James Watt in 1763 CE, which kick-started the Industrial Revolution. The proliferation of newspapers and books in the 19th century was based on large-scale industrial production of paper to meet growing demands.

88 Gunpowder

Gunpowder was invented by the Chinese around 850 CE, when alchemists were tinkering around with medical potions that, they hoped, could extend the human lifespan.

1 Gunpowder was discovered when saltpetre (potassium nitrate) was accidentally mixed with sulphur and charcoal. This resulted in smoke and flames burning down a whole house. The Song dynasty that ruled from 960 to 1279 CE used gunpowder to thwart the Mongol attacks on China. During the next few centuries, Chinese perfected many more gunpowder-based weapons.

2 Until the 13th century CE, gunpowder remained a monopoly of the Chinese, but it was passed on to Europeans and to the Islamic world via the Silk Road. This started a period called the 'Era of Islamic Gunpowder Empires', between the 14th and 18th centuries, when Islamic dynasties such as the Ottomans, Safavids and Mughals conquered vast territories using gunpowder-based weapons. The Ottoman Turks used cannons filled

with gunpowder to breach the famed impregnable walls of Constantinople in 1453 CE, thereby ending the European monopoly over trade routes. In 1526 CE, in the First Battle of Panipat, Babur deployed gunpowder-based firearms to conquer the powerful Delhi Sultanate.

3 In Europe, meanwhile, they employed the bell-casting technology used in constructing churches and cathedrals to build bronze and wrought-iron cannons. The Europeans used gunpowder, along with cannons, in their conquest of the New World. Thus, gunpowder altered the course of military history across the western and eastern worlds.

MING DYNASTY EARLY CANNON THAT COULD FIRE CAST-IRON BALLS FILLED WITH GUNPOWDER

89 Compass

A device that helps determine direction, the compass was an important invention that enabled navigation and many other events in history.

1 Before the compass was invented, mariners determined geographical positions primarily using landmarks and celestial bodies. The first compasses are thought to have been introduced during the Han dynasty of China, as early as the first century CE, primarily for spiritual and divination-related activities. It was then referred to as the 'South pointing fish'. During the Chinese golden age of the Song dynasty, around 1040 CE, compasses started to be used for maritime navigation purposes. The technology was then passed on to the Yuan dynasty during the early 13th century.

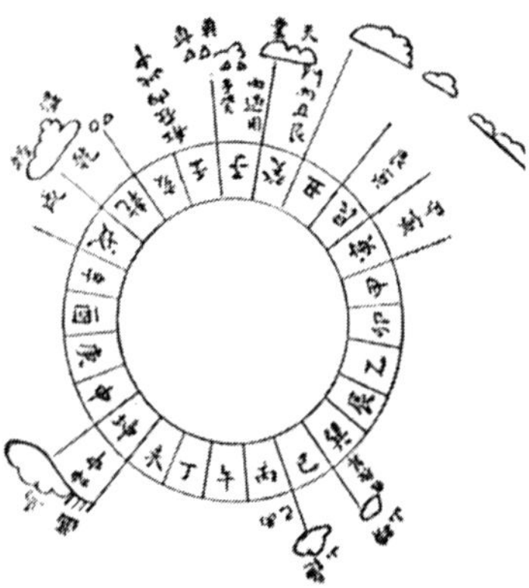

ANCIENT CHINESE COMPASS

2 In Europe, during the latter half of the 12th century, there were descriptions of magnetized needles being used to direct lost ships. However, it was around 1300 CE that in Europe and in the Islamic world, compasses started making an appearance.

3 From the beginning of the 15th century until the middle of the 20th century, compasses enabled western European nations, initially led by the Portuguese and Spanish, to explore, conquer and colonize several lands, most of them previously unknown to them.

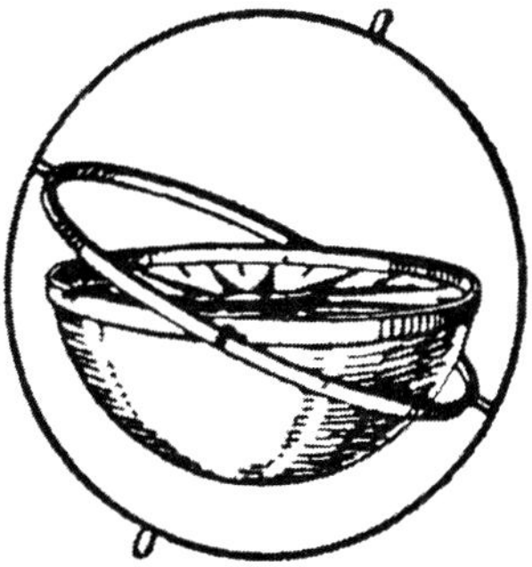

EARLY MODERN DRY COMPASS SUSPENDED BY A GIMBAL (1570)

90

Printing Press

The printing press was invented by a German goldsmith named Johannes Gutenberg around 1440 CE.

1 Woodblock printing was invented in China in the 9th century. Korean bookmakers were printing with moveable metal types a century before Gutenberg, but it was Gutenberg who achieved the first print run of 200 copies of the Bible in Latin. He printed these in a period of three years, a comparatively high speed during those times of hand-copied manuscripts.

2 The Gutenberg printing press accelerated the European Renaissance movement, which was already in motion for about a century. The invention enabled the faster sharing and dissemination of knowledge. For example, ships from Venice not only carried Bibles and Christian literature, but also important news to distant ports across the world. Local printers copied these and handed them to riders who then distributed these across towns and villages. The Gutenberg

press also played a large role in the Reformation movement. After German theologian and religious reformer Martin Luther nailed his 'Ninety-five Theses' encapsulating the propositions for what became Protestantism later, to the church door in Wittenberg on 31 October 1517, the printing press enabled this to be printed as far as London. Martin Luther became the world's first bestselling author and his writings accounted for a third of all books sold in Germany. The invention of the printing press also laid the foundation for the Scientific Revolution, as new scientific findings and experimental data were printed and shared with many more people.

EARLY PRINTING PRESS, 1872

3 The printing press enabled a new era through democratization of cultural, religious, and scientific information, which was until then monopolized by the elites in different social, cultural or academic spheres.

GUTENBERG (FAR RIGHT) AT HIS PRESS

91 Galileo Galilei

Referred to as the 'father of modern science', Galileo Galilei was Italian astronomer, philosopher and mathematician. He was born in Pisa, Italy, and lived from 1564 to 1642 CE.

GALILEO GALILEI, A PORTRAIT

1 Though Galileo initially enrolled in a monastery, he decided to move out to study medicine and then mathematics. During his initial career, he formulated some theorems on the centre of gravity, which gained him recognition. As a result, he got an appointment as the chair of mathematics in the University of Pisa. Here, using the Leaning Tower of Pisa as a demonstration site, he showed that the speed of the fall of an object was not proportional to its weight. By 1609 CE, he formulated the law of falling bodies.

2 During this time, Galileo was introduced to an early form of telescope that he improved upon. He then joined the University of Padua. He discovered four moons of Jupiter and the phases of Venus. Through these, Galileo posited that the Sun is the centre of the universe and that Earth is a planet, as Copernicus had argued earlier. But this finding brought him into a direct clash with the ideals of the Church, which blamed Galileo for attempting to reinterpret the Bible. The Church later condemned Galileo to imprisonment.

3 Galileo's insistence on scientific experiments to disprove popular beliefs and the usage of mathematics, rather than subjective accounts to explain natural phenomena, established the foundations of scientific methodology. His discovery of the telescope revolutionized the world of astronomy.

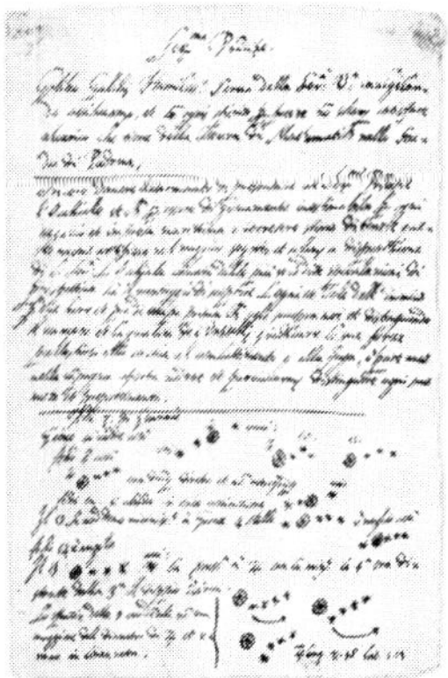

GALILEO'S NOTES ON HIS OBSERVATION OF THE MOONS OF JUPITER

92 Isaac Newton

One of the great physicists and mathematicians in history, Isaac Newton discovered the laws of motion and the theory of gravity. He was born in 1643 CE IN Lincolnshire, UK, and died in 1727 CE.

1 Newton had lost his father even before he was born, and his mother got remarried when he was a child. He was interested in mathematics and mechanics from a young age. He attended Trinity College, Cambridge, when the Scientific Revolution was in its advanced stages, with contributions from scientists, such as Copernicus, Kepler, and Galileo.

ISAAC NEWTON, A PORTRAIT

2 Newton was influenced by the works of Rene Descartes during this period, and he discovered the binomial theorem and developed the mathematical study of calculus. As the Great Plague consumed London,

Newton immersed himself into his study of the solar system. Then he joined as a fellow at Trinity College, Cambridge, where he proposed the theory of colour, that white light was a composite of all the colours. In 1687, after years of intense study, Newton published his most important work, the *Philosophiae Naturalis Principia Mathematica*. This book outlined the three basic laws of motion, which then enabled him to explain the theory of gravity.

3 Newton was a member of the British Parliament representing Cambridge University for two years, though he was not active. He was made president of the Royal Society in 1703 CE and was knighted two years later. With Newton, the Scientific Revolution reached its pinnacle. His work laid the foundations for modern physics, modern physical optics and mathematics.

NEWTON'S OWN COPY OF *PRINCIPIA*

93 Steam Engine

Though the idea of the steam engine was modified several times in the past, a smoothly working and efficient model was invented by James Watt.

1 Hero of Alexandria, a Greco-Egyptian mathematician, had published a description of a steam-powered device called the 'Hero engine' during the early half of the first century CE. However, it was only in the 17th century that the power of steam was harnessed in a practical way. In 1698, British inventor Thomas Savery patented a steam power pump, which was improved upon by James Watt with the support of Matthew Boulton, between 1763 and 1775 CE. Compared to the earlier design, Watt's design was more efficient.

JAMES WATT, A PORTRAIT

2 The invention of the efficient steam engine ushered in the Industrial Revolution. Until then horses and mules were used to transport goods from mines and textile mills, both of which were slow and inefficient processes. Steam engines improved productivity, efficiency and speed, both in the industrial process and in transportation. Once steam technology was applied to road vehicles, locomotives and boats, it was possible to transport large loads of goods to the cities and factories at a fraction of the earlier cost.

3 With the advent of the steam engine, Europe and the United States of America saw an incredible growth in the transportation of goods and people. This unravelled a series of positive changes across the economy – enabling better work, life and market efficiencies.

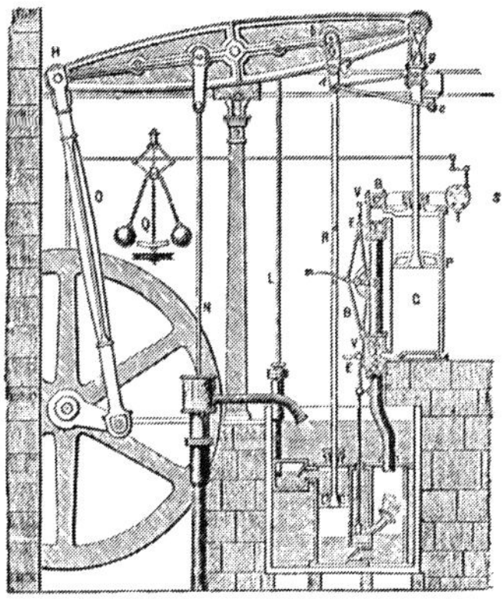

EARLY DRAWING OF THE BOULTON AND WATT STEAM ENGINE

94 Vaccination

Vaccination is a process by which an external vaccine containing a weakened virus is administered, thereby stimulating our body's immune system to protect it against infectious diseases.

1 There is evidence that, as early as 1500 CE, Chinese and Indian physicians employed inoculation, by grinding smallpox scabs and blowing them into the patient's nose through a tube, to fight against the variola virus that caused smallpox. In the early 18th century, as Lady Montagu, the wife of the British ambassador to the Ottoman Empire travelled across Constantinople, she observed this process of inoculation known as 'variolation', which was by then practised there. She submitted her son for inoculation against smallpox and advocated for the procedure on her return to Europe.

2 In 1796, a British physician called Edward Jenner started experimenting with variola. At that time, smallpox was killing more than 10 per cent of the population. Jenner's observation was that milkmaids were generally immune to smallpox due

to the blisters they developed from the cowpox virus called the cowpox vaccinia virus. Jenner scraped cowpox blisters from a milkmaid and on 14 May 1796, he inoculated an eight-year-old boy, thus saving him from a full-blown infection. This inoculation process, using a virus as a vaccine, eventually became the common term for this process – vaccination. The success of this experiment soon spread across Europe by the early 1800s. Napoleon, who was at war with Britain during that time, had all his French troops vaccinated.

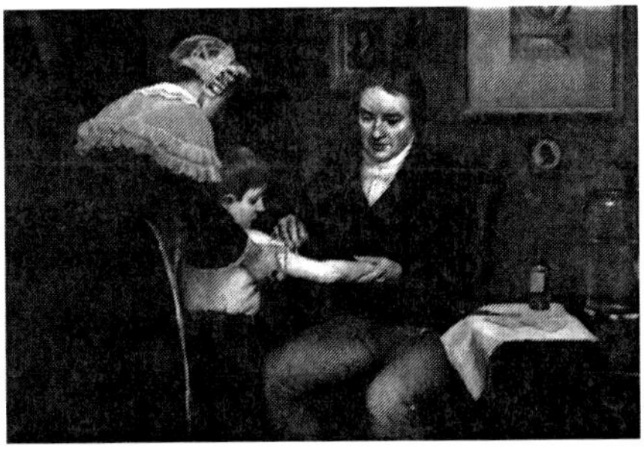

JENNER'S FIRST VACCINATION ON EIGHT-YEAR-OLD JAMES PHIPPS ON 14 MAY 1796

3 Jenner is credited with having saved more lives than anyone else in history. Smallpox, which killed 300 million people in the 20th century itself, was eradicated in 1980 through consistent vaccination programmes across the world. Vaccines have since been developed against several infectious diseases like tetanus, influenza, mumps, diphtheria, whooping cough, polio, measles and rubella.

95

Charles Darwin

A British biologist and naturalist, Charles Darwin is credited with developing the theory of evolution. He lived from 1809 to 1882 CE.

1 Darwin was born in a wealthy family, where his father was a medical doctor and his grandfather a botanist. He was initially a student at the University of Edinburgh and then at Christ's College, Cambridge. After he graduated, one of his professors recommended Darwin to the position of a naturalist on an exploration ship, the HMS *Beagle*, which was getting ready to take a five-year trip around the world.

CHARLES DARWIN, A PORTRAIT

2 The HMS *Beagle* started its expedition in 1831. Among the territories explored were the Pacific Islands and Galapagos Archipelago, which gave Darwin the opportunity to observe birds, animals and plants closely, and collect specimens

and fossils. As he continued travelling, he started noticing variations in the same species across different geographies. Upon his return to England in 1836, he presented his findings in the *Journal of Researches*. Darwin formed a broad theory of natural selection, and for several years continued to do extensive research and experiments, including selective breeding of plants and animals, and seeking more evidence to support this. In 1842 CE, he drafted a 35-page summary of his theory of natural selection, but did not publish as he feared that would amount to blasphemy. However, in the 1850s, Darwin started to write his detailed book, which was eventually published in 1859 CE, known as *On the Origin of Species*.

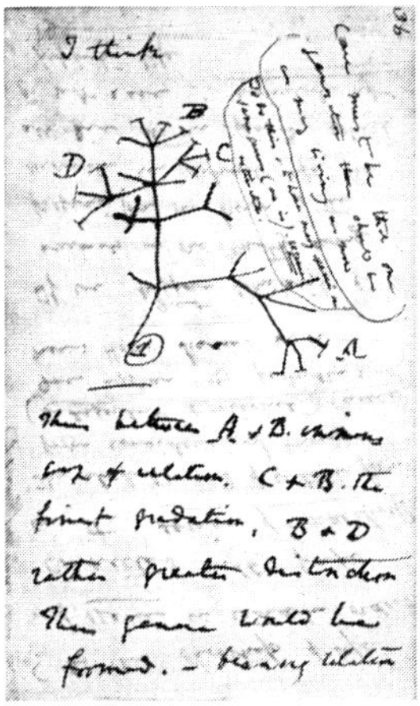

NOTES ON *TRANSMUTATION OF SPECIES* AND DARWIN'S FIRST EVOLUTIONARY TREE

3 Charles Darwin is now regarded as one of the most important scientists of modern times, with the whole field of evolutionary biology founded on his work and efforts being made to study why his work is essential to understanding the place of human beings in this world. Darwin was buried in Westminster Abbey in London, UK.

96 Sigmund Freud

Sigmund Freud was the founder of psychoanalysis, a branch of medical science that gives insights into human behaviour and treating mental health conditions. He lived from 1856 to 1939 CE.

1 Freud was born in the Austrian town of Freiberg and then moved to Vienna, from where he received his medical degree. He then started his practice in treating medical illnesses in a systematic fashion. He was also influenced by his friend, Josef Breuer, a physician and pioneer of neuroanalysis.

SIGMUND FREUD

2 Freud later developed his psychoanalytic theory: he proposed that neuroses had their origins in traumatic experiences that his patients had gone through in the past. According to him, though these experiences seem to be forgotten and submerged

in the subconscious, recalling them back to consciousness is important for getting rid of the neurotic symptoms completely. He published a number of books on psychoanalysis, including the *Studies in Hysteria* and *The Interpretation of Dreams*, where he explored theories of Dream Analysis, Id, Ego, Super Ego and Psychic Energy.

3 Initially, many prominent thinkers of the time did not give importance to Freud's theories, but after the publication of his book, *Five Lectures on Psycho-Analysis*, in 1916, his fame grew across the world. He fled from Vienna to escape from the Nazi regime and eventually took his own life in 1939, while he was in England.

97

Telephone

The telephone is one of the greatest innovations in communication technology.

1 In 1664 CE, Robert Hooke, an English scientist, conducted several communication experiments with cans and a string and created the first acoustic telephone. Centuries later, in 1838 CE, Samuel Morse, American inventor, developed an electric telegraph that could transmit messages. In 1861 CE, a self-taught German inventor Philip Reis, created the first working telephone model. He created the first make-and-break telephone, today called the Reis telephone. His device could capture sound, convert it into electrical impulses and then transmit it through electrical wires to another device. Reis named his device the 'telephon'.

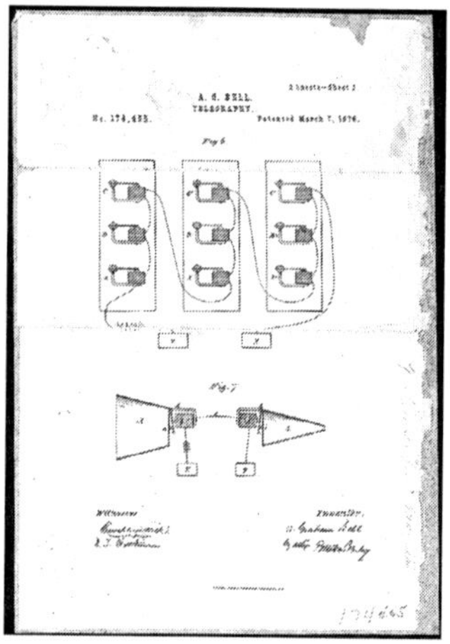

BELL'S PHONE PATENT

2 In early 1870s, Alexander Graham Bell, a Scottish-born scientist, started working on a harmonic telegraph - to simultaneously transmit multiple messages over a wire. In 1876, Bell patented his telephone model, though other scientists including Antonio Meucci and Elisha Grey were also working on similar technologies. Bell then set up the Bell Telephone company, now known as AT&T. During the same year, the first telephone exchange was set up by Hungarian engineer Tivadar Puskas. By the early 1900s, rotary dial phones started becoming popular.

3 In 1948, the transistor, a semiconductor device, considered to be the building block of modern electronics, was developed. This paved the way for the development of the smartphone. In 1973, Motorola, an American company developed and demonstrated cellular phones, which began the era of mobile phones. The first smartphones were introduced in the market in 1993.

BELL IN 1892, CALLING CHICAGO FROM NEW YORK, USA

98 Electricity

Electricity can easily be dubbed as the backbone of modern society, enabling a variety of applications, such as in transport, communication and lighting.

1 Ancient texts from 2700 BCE, during the time of the Third Dynasty of Egypt, talk about an electric fish and the 'shocks' they gave. Thales of Miletus, a pre-Socratic Greek mathematician and philosopher, during 500 BCE, discovered that static electricity could be generated by rubbing amber rods on cat fur. The Baghdad Battery, discovered in present-day Khujut Rabu, Iraq, which included a ceramic pot, a copper tube and an iron rod, dated back to around 2,000 years, is believed to have been a battery, though its original purpose is still unclear. Later in 1675 CE, the English physicist Robert Boyle published a book about the production of electricity.

2 In 1752 CE, scientist Benjamin Franklin, one of the founding fathers of the United States of America, conducted extensive research on electricity, by tying a key to a kite during a thunderstorm to prove that static electricity and

lightning were one and the same thing. In 1831 CE, Michael Faraday, an English scientist, discovered the principles of electromagnetic induction, which formed the foundation of today's electricity generation. In 1879 CE, Thomas Alva Edison, an American scientist, invented the incandescent electric light bulb that revolutionized domestic electricity usage. Meanwhile, in 1887 CE, Nicola Tesla, a Serbian-American inventor, developed an induction motor that ran on alternating current (AC), challenging the direct current (DC) thesis promoted by Edison and changing the way we transfer current. Tesla also designed the first hydroelectric power plant at the Niagara Falls in the USA, where electric power was transmitted from the Niagara Falls to Buffalo (around 37.5 km).

AN ENGRAVING ABOUT BENJAMIN FRANKLIN'S THEORIES

3 Today, most of the electricity in the world is produced using fossil fuels like coal, petroleum and natural gas. However, there is an increased awareness of greenhouse gas emissions from fossil fuels, and renewable energy, such as wind and hydel power, is being explored.

99

Albert Einstein

Considered among the greatest physicists of all time, Albert Einstein was born in 1879 CE in Germany and lived until 1955 CE.

1 Einstein's family moved to Munich when he was just six months old, and later to Italy. Though his father wanted him to pursue electrical engineering, Einstein resented the rote method of learning in school. At a young age itself he was interested in mathematics and physics, and as a 12-year-old, he taught himself Euclidean geometry and formulated his own proof to the Pythagorean theorem. He graduated from the Swiss Federal Polytechnic School in Zurich and then joined as an assistant examiner at the patent office, since he could not secure a teaching position.

ALBERT EINSTEIN IN 1921

2 After his PhD, Einstein was appointed as a lecturer and (in 1914 CE) as a professor in the University of Berlin. As a physicist, he tried to reconcile Newtonian mechanics with electromagnetism, and his special theory of relativity stemmed from that. His studies on the thermal properties of light laid the basis of the photon theory. In the 1920s, he worked on unified field theories and the interpretation of quantum theory. In 1921, he received the Nobel Prize in physics. As Nazism swept across Germany, Einstein, a Jew, gave up his German citizenship and immigrated to the USA to join Princeton University as a professor.

3 After the Second World War, Einstein was involved in the World Government Movement, where he championed the cause of global governance after the atomic bombing of Japan. In 1952, he was offered the presidency of Israel, which he declined. He died from internal bleeding, for which he refused surgery, not wishing to prolong his life artificially.

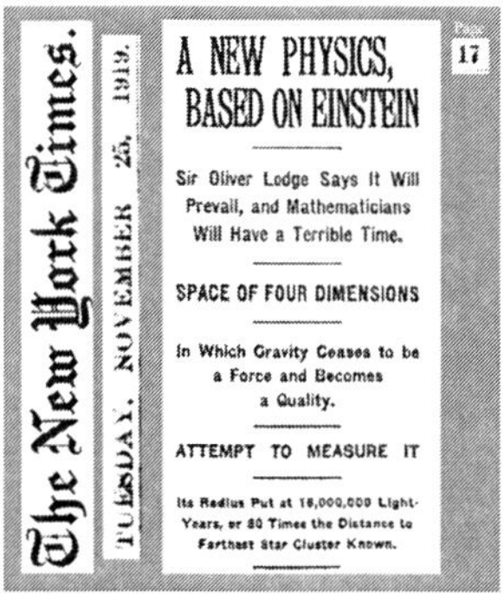

The New York Times.

TUESDAY, NOVEMBER 25, 1919.

Page 17

A NEW PHYSICS, BASED ON EINSTEIN

Sir Oliver Lodge Says It Will Prevail, and Mathematicians Will Have a Terrible Time.

SPACE OF FOUR DIMENSIONS

In Which Gravity Ceases to be a Force and Becomes a Quality.

ATTEMPT TO MEASURE IT

Its Radius Put at 18,000,000 Light-Years, or 80 Times the Distance to Farthest Star Cluster Known.

THE NEW YORK TIMES PUBLISHED A REPORT CONFIRMING EINSTEIN'S THEORY

100

Aviation

Aviation has fascinated human beings throughout history. In Hindu mythology there are many flying beings and the mention of a 'Pushpak', a flying vessel, and in Greek mythology too, there is Icarus, a mythical boy who flew in the sky.

1 During the Renaissance and the Scientific Revolution, Leonardo da Vinci, Galileo Galilei and Isaac Newton helped to develop an initial understanding of aerodynamics. During the early 18th century, Swiss mathematician David Bernoulli defined the relationship between pressure, density and velocity, thereby simplifying the understanding of aerodynamic forces.

2 In 1783 CE, the Montgolfier brothers initially sent up an unmanned hot-air balloon, which flew over Annonay, France, followed by a manned one. Then almost a century later, in 1890 CE, the inventor Clement Ader made a short flight over 50 metres and just about 20 centimetres above the ground, a significant breakthrough in aviation. Wilbur and Orville Wright, two brothers from the

United States of America, who had experimented passionately with building aircraft, on 17 December 1903, successfully made the first sustained, controlled, powered, manned flight in history. They made four attempts, the longest of which lasted 59 seconds and covered 852 feet.

MONTGOLFIER BROTHERS' FIRST HOT-AIR BALLOON

3 In the following years, airplanes started to acquire widespread recognition. In 1914 CE, the world's first scheduled passenger air service started in Florida, USA. After the Second World War ended, civil aviation experienced rapid growth as many cities built their own airports. Currently, flight technology has incorporated digital and even artificial intelligence aspects.

WRIGHT BROTHERS' FIRST FLIGHT, 1903

101

Penicillin

Penicillin was discovered by Scottish scientist Sir Alexander Fleming in 1928 CE, revolutionizing the field of healthcare.

1 Alexander Fleming was experimenting with the flu virus in St Mary's Hospital in London, when he went on two weeks' leave. As he returned, he found that a green mould called *Penicillium notatum* had contaminated and killed some of the bacteria he had been growing. He isolated and experimented with this mould, and its effects on different bacteria. However, initially, his discovery was not considered useful in any way by his colleagues.

2 Until the early 20th century, infections from injuries, surgical procedures and cuts were considered fatal. People died while working in their backyards and in battles, since there were no antibacterial medicines available. This discovery of Fleming changed all of that. It was formally named penicillin in March 1929. Almost a decade later, an Oxford pathologist and another British biochemist, Howard Florey, expanded on Fleming's research,

SIR ALEXANDER FLEMING

vigorously growing and purifying penicillin. By 1942 CE, there was worldwide interest in penicillin, by which time an injectable mass-produced medicine was made ready.

3 During the Second World War, penicillin helped reduce infections and amputations, and even helped prevent death. Fleming received the Nobel Prize in medicine in 1945. Now, penicillin is the most widely used antibiotic in the world.

Selected Bibliography

Asif, M.A. 2016. *A Book of Conquest: The Chachnama and Muslim Origins in South Asia*. Cambridge, Massachusetts: Harvard University Press.

Edited by Baker, Matt and John Andrews, J. 2020. *Timelines of World History: Chart the Course of History through Ages*. California: Thunder Bay Press.

Baur, S.W. 2007. *The History of the Ancient World: From the Earliest Accounts to the Fall of Rome*. New York: W. W. Norton & Company.

Bryson, B. 2003. *A Short History of Nearly Everything*. New York: Broadway Books.

Bynum, W.F. 2013. *A Little History of Science*. New Haven and London: Yale University Press.

Gernet, J, Foster, J.R and Hartman, C. 2008. *A History of Chinese People*. New York: Cambridge University Press.

Hart-Davis, A. 2007. *History: From the Dawn of the Civilization to the Present Day*. London. DK Books.

Head, T. 2017. *World History 101: A Crash Course in the History of the World*. New York: Simon & Schuster.

Lowe, N. 2013. *Mastering Modern World History*. London: Bloomsbury.

Morison, S.E, 1965. *The Oxford History of the American People*. New York: Oxford University Press.

Overy, R. 2015. *The Times Complete History of the World*. London: William Collins.

Singh, U. 2009. *Ancient India: From Stone Age to the 12th Century*. New Delhi: Pearson Education India.

Smithsonian History Year by Year: The History of the World from Stone Age to the Digital Age. 2013. New York and London: DK Children.

Sutherland, J. 2013. *A Little History of Literature*. New Haven and London: Yale University Press.

Thapar, R. 2003. *A History of India, Vol 1, From Origins to 1300*. New Delhi: Penguin India.

Taylor, A. 2008. *The Rise and Fall of the Great Empires*. London: Quercus Publishing.

Weatherford, J. 2005. *Genghis Khan and the Making of the Modern World*. New York: Crown Publishers.

Winks, R.W. 1992. *A History of Civilization*. New Jersey: Prentice Hall.

Wood, M. 2020. *The Story of China: A Portrait of a Civilisation and its People*. London: Simon & Schuster.

Websites Accessed:

BBC.co.uk; Biography.com; Britannica.com; History.com; Khanacademy.org; Livescience.com; Nationalgeography.com; Wikipedia.org; Worldhistory.org

IMAGE COPYRIGHT INFORMATION AND SOURCES

THE NOUN PROJECT: Page 1: *bottom, clockwise from top left*: Qutub Minar: Eucalyp; Sri Maiamman Temple: Vectors Point; Throne: Eucalyp; Taj Mahal: Berkah Icon; **Page 41:** *top, clockwise from top right*: Angkor Wat: Start Up Grap; Forbidden City: mynamepong; Borobudur: Brickclay; **Page 59:** *bottom, left to right:* Hagia Sophia: Lluisa Iborra; Hero: Anton; Iran Mosque: Olena Panasovska; Landmark Genghis Khan Statue: Ary Prasetyo; **Page 87:** *top, clockwise from top left*: African: Smallliket; African Shield: Made; Timbuktu: Linseed Studio; African elephant: Alejandro Capellan; **Page 107:** *bottom, clockwise from top left*: Aztec: Eucalyp; Olmec Head: Alberto Guerra Quintinalla; Kukulcan: Jake Dunham; Mask: IconMark; **Page 127:** *top, clockwise from left*: Florence: Start Up Grap; Russia: supalerk laipa; Windsor Castle: Chanut is Industries; Samurai: Andre Buand; **Page 159:** *top, left to right*: Architect: Lutfi Gani Al A; Artist: Ben Avery; Painting: Hamel Khale; Skyscraper: Komkrit Noen; **Page 183:** *bottom, clockwise from top left*: Piano: Ayub Irawan; Writing: Royal Icon; Poet: Webtechops LLP; Writer: Hey Rabbit; **Page 209:** *top, clockwise from top left*: Compass: zainul arifin; Locomotive Train: Vectors Point; Wright Brothers: HeadOfBirds; Telephone: Evon

Page 36: *The Rulers of the Mughal Dynasty from Babur to Aurangzeb, with their Ancestor Timur:* Attribution: Khalili Collections / CC-BY-SA 3.0 IGO; https://commons.wikimedia.org/ wiki/ File:Khalili_Collection_Islamic_Art_mss_0874.3.jpg

FREEPIK.COM: Pages 1, 59, 107, 183 (all top), **159** (bottom): ZigZag and **Pages 41, 87, 127, 209:** bottom graphic

PIXABAY: Page 18: Shore Temple: c2squareinc; **Page 33:** Vijay Narasimha; **Page 44:** Deepu Joseph; **Page 61:** UmmePhotos; **Page 101 (top):** mel_88; **Page 108:** Erica Vicente; **Page 111:** angel chavez; **Page 115:** dexal B; **Page 118:** Monica Neumann; **Page 125:** Poswiecie; **Page 151:** Kiryha_rigel; **Page 166:** Adri Marie; **Page 176:** pEXELS

Acknowledgements

Thank you:

- My grandparents – mummy and daddy, ammamma and appappa.
- Vatsala Kaul Banerjee. For her vision and dedication. I owe this series to her.
- Pradipti Jayaram. For her careful and caring edits.
- Rajalaxmi Pradhan. For meticulously proofreading.
- Sunil Rajshekhar, V. Raghunathan, Ferose V.R., Amit Gopal and Dipali Sikand. For opening doors of greater opportunities for me.
- Krishna – Bookworm, Bangalore. For my first book signing experience.
- Vidyadhar Prabhudesai, Saurabh Nanda and Abraham Paul Vadakkancherry. For introducing me to public talks.
- Aunty Nimmy Paul. For her diehard support.
- My friends – Sammy, Aditya, Siddhar, Ura, Isa and Johan.
- My godparents. Cousins Sarah and Isaac.
- My aunts. My uncles. My cousins.
- My friends. My well-wishers.
- My school. My teachers.